CYBER SHADOWS
Power, Crime, and Hacking Everyone

D1515000

CYBER SHADOWS
Power, Crime, and Hacking Everyone

by

Carolyn Nordstrom & Lisa Carlson

CYBER SHADOWS
Power, Crime, and Hacking Everyone

10 9 8 7 6 5 4 3 2

ISBN: 978-0-9912451-0-9

Distributed by ACTA Publications
4848 N. Clark Street, Chicago, IL 60640.
800-397-2282, www.actapublications.com

Published by
CORBY BOOKS
A Division of Corby Publishing, LP
P.O. Box 93
Notre Dame, IN 46556
Editorial Office: (574) 784-3482

Manufactured in the United States of America

TABLE OF CONTENTS

ACKNOWLEDGMENTS

MOST IMPORTANTLY, we'd like to thank Michael—he is the reason for this book.

Brian Krebs, Charlie Miller, Gene Spafford, Tiago Cardieri, Mark, and two who preferred to remain anonymous enriched this work with interviews.

The book grew with the kind help and patient explanations of Bruce Schneier, Jonathan Broussard, Chris Paget, Stefano Zanero, Drew Porter, Dan Kaminsky, Scott Shackelford, Joshua Corman, Mark Stechschulte, Christine Dudley, Marc Goodman, Tarik Nesh-Nash, Marc Rodgers, Dual Core (who won the 2012 Def-Con music award and talked with me about tech and music), Todd Agers, Kevin Estis, Zachary Julian, Jared Schneider, Don Bailey, Fred Go, and the many people who helped us and preferred to remain anonymous.

Their wisdom and quotes deepen the book.

Sal Moya brought abstract words to vibrant life with his art, which graces the cover.

CAROLYN: My deepest thanks go to the Nurse, aka Brad Smith, who taught me the ropes (including telling me I dressed like crap and to wear proper hacker-conference clothes) at my first Blackhat and DefCon conferences. He is fondly remembered by many: Nurse collapsed onstage in 2013 while giving his talk at a conference and passed away shortly after.

Thanks as well to David Sidel who told me to go to DefCon; to the BlackHat organizers for media passes two years; to UND OIT who kept rebuilding my devices; and especially to Professor Aaron Striegel and Dirk Van Bruggen in Electrical Engineering Computer Security, who took me on as a student—this book owes much to their excellent and remarkably patient mentoring.

My students at the University of Notre Dame have been amazing: making video trailers for this book, web presentations on the topic, and good counsel.

Lisa is one of the best authors I've worked with: she is a wellspring of creativity and responsibility—endless thanks.

LISA: I would like thank Gail, Jon, Brian, and Bridget Carlson for their support; to John and Una Majeska for their encouragement; to Missy Fandel, Taylor Roberts, Katie Heit, Nick Hamilton, Gabrielle Going, and John Stabile for listening to me talk about cybercrime for hours on end; and to Donna, François, Isabelle, Claire, and Luke Madath for their stories and insight.

Above all, I would like to thank Carolyn Nordstrom for not only letting me in on this project, but also guiding me through the process. I never could have done this without her.

Hearty thanks to Jim Langford, Tim Carroll and Eileen Carroll at Corby Press. After five books with academic presses, people ask me why we chose an independent "family-run" press. Corby gave us remarkable freedom and support to make core decisions that are generally unheard of at large presses; and their turn-around time for contracting, copy-editing and proofs-to-publication runs in weeks—not months or years. Corby was Lisa's first choice from the beginning: it represents many Millennial values: local, personal, innovative relationships. We noticed many cyber literati follow this publishing route.

After we turned our manuscript over to Jim, Lisa and I coincidentally read a piece written by him: "Unless You Become Like Children." In this, Jim talks about how, after their own children were grown, he and his wife began adopting children others did not: biracial kids with severe learning disabilities. He and his wife bought a farmhouse on fifteen acres in the country and began running camps for disadvantaged inner-city youth, most who experienced violence, poverty, drugs, and abuse. Ten years ago they averaged thirty-five hundred children and eighteen hundred volunteer visitors yearly. That night Lisa texted me: "We made the right choice in Press."

OPENING

MICHAEL
12-YEAR-OLD BOY IN AIRPORT, TRAVELING ALONE
OCTOBER 12, 2011
~ CN ~

MY FLIGHT WAS GROUNDED at O'Hare Airport due to mechanical problems. All the passengers were at the gate waiting; no one knew when we'd be able to go. I noticed a boy traveling alone without anything to eat, and decided to take him a sandwich if he was hungry. So he wouldn't feel like "some kid needing a handout," I mentioned the U.S. military drones recently hacked in Afghanistan, and said I was curious what people his age thought about things like this—were they: "No, didn't see that coming," or not too surprised given their knowledge of tech? He began talking without a pause:

"I'm not surprised at all.

"I mean you can hack the DS [Nintendo], playing games on-line; you can download a program, an app, from the Internet to DS that turns your computer into a phone, even into a landline.

"It doesn't mean I can do it, but everyone my age knows this stuff. It's super easy to hack—to hack all this.

"You can get fake credit cards online to get an account on the games. Most every kid knows this, whether they do it or not.

"Then there's the grid-decoding programs you can get for encryption, or like for codes, binary. Here's how it works: The code is laid out in a grid and it has these numbers—codes in each box on the grid—and like for a 0 you code this other code in [gives examples], box by box, and you crack it.

"It's not just games. Hacking into government sites is a piece of cake for some. It's the same kind of thing—you use the same kinds of tools you can get off the Internet. Kids my age, there are some that this is so easy for. Everybody knows someone like this, hears about it, at school. It's like it's not a big deal.

"Like the 'friend of a friend of a friend,' well, he can hack 3000 PayPal cash—can do it like nothing.

"All security systems are real similar. To access any, you have to send a virus to take over, to take control, of the security systems. And the Grid.

"Look, the way you go about hacking games, it's a similar kind of thing to hack into places to get money, or whatever you want. It's the same kind of thinking, the same kinds of approaches. Take what someone learns about hacking a game, and then take it up a level, apply it, and that's how you get into a bank.

"People can hack into banks and take money, and no one knows. It happens all the time; it's not hard. Sony got hacked a couple months ago.

"I mean, people can even hack the Big Red Button."

He flops back in his chair—a raw expression on his face, like a clear understanding of inevitability, of being way too young for this but unable to avoid it. Struck by his expression, I asked him how he sees the future.

"The Future? I'm ready for what's to come—it's not going to be good. I know that it's going to be chaos.

"I call it The Chaos—the time of The Chaos."

I ask him, "What will The Chaos be like for you?"

"If I know what I'm doing—if I'm smart and if I have a safe spot to be during The Chaos—I'll be ok. I'll make it through.

"I mean, they've already invented a microchip with all identity info, GPS, all that—stuff small enough to be like a camera in your bloodstream. Chips for people are more advanced, but like what you put in your dog. The Bible even talks about this—called the mark of the beast."

"What's the future of this?" I ask.

"Hackers will pretty much take over the computer systems. They'll be in charge, and they'll do what they want; set things up the way they want it in the world. They control it all. Everything. That's just how it is now, they *are* the power."

Michael sat up, looked me in the eyes, and said:

"What's the matter with you adults? This is all obvious; it's all around us."

He paused, and then said with the utmost seriousness:

"You adults see all this, and you do Nothing.

"You do nothing to fix this, and we'll all suffer because of this. You close your eyes to it.

"It's worse than that. You all show exactly the wrong solutions—what will make it all worse. It's like with the movies. There's a ton of movies on crises and the Apocalypse. And they always show some guy getting a gun and going off by himself—dealing with everything all solitary, killing for food, running around with his big guns blasting away.

"People are so dumb" [*and here he clearly means adults*]. "They don't show that people need to create communities to survive. People aren't going to make it running around with their guns all on their own. There's only one way to make it, and why aren't you adults talking about this?

"Movies on the Apocalypse should be showing that when the crisis hits, the need will be rebuilding humanity, starting a new life, working together as communities. You know, caring.

"People don't understand what they are seeing. They think tomorrow's going to be a good day. They don't see that someone can hack nuclear weapons. Remember the Cold War: If you push a button, I will push a button. Well, now someone can do that with the push of a button at home."

"How do you deal with this?" I asked. I meant both how do we as a world begin to solve this; and also, how does he—a 12-year-old boy, seeing this in a world where adults ignore what's in front of their eyes—deal with these truths?

Without missing a beat, as if he had thought this through in the past, Michael said:

"Hack the hack.

"Rewrite the system. Repair control. Create and send viruses to the infected computers so you can control and stop what's going on.

"It's gotta stop. Already you can assassinate someone from a computer—like for example a weapon controlled by a phone activated by a computer and its links.

"I want to create an unhackable hack for security systems. Codes in the motherboard.

"Not many in the older generations get this at all. What happens if we are planning an anti-terrorist campaign and the terrorists hack this and get all the plans and thousands of our troops and men and women and children die because of this? We have to fix this—an unhackable hack.

"No one [*speaking of his generation*] trusts the FBI and CIA. Not at all! They lie! They know stuff we need to know to survive. And they don't tell us. They hide all this and they'll let us die, and not tell us what we need to know to survive. No, I'm not like them. I'm ethical.

"It kinda feels like dealing with this all in the future falls on us—us kids. But we know what to do. We've been reading on this, watching all the movies, watching what's going on—thinking about it."

CAROLYN

THIS BOOK CAME TO LIFE the minute Michael looked me in the eye and said: "You adults are doing Nothing. The Chaos is coming and you adults do *Nothing*. You just make it worse."

A random event popped into my mind. Before I embarked on this trip, an undergraduate student I had never met walked into my office saying she wanted to learn to do research and did I need any assistance? Lots of students ask this, far more than I can ever work with.

After listening to Michael, I pulled out my cell phone and texted the student—whom I knew nothing about—that we were doing a book together. Lisa was just starting her sophomore year at the University of Notre Dame and had never taken an anthropology class. Nor, she promptly texted back, did she know anything about computers beyond being in the first generation of digital natives. Perfect, I responded, you can write about what it's like to become an adult walking into the realities of the unfolding digital world and its shadows.

=✳=

Michael's story reached out to pull in one other person that day in O'Hare Airport. As Michael was finishing his explanation of "The Chaos," I realized that a man sitting across from the two of us was staring at Michael with an intensity and amazement that seemed to momentarily override normal public decorum. The man was in his mid- to late-20s, dressed in pressed khaki slacks and a polo shirt, had a short groomed haircut, and sat upright in a way that suggested a comfortable authority and professionalism.

I turned to him, still in amazement myself, and said, "You must have been listening too."

But I didn't exist to him. He said to Michael:

> "I can't believe you just said that. I can't believe you used the words 'The Chaos.'
>
> "This is my work—security. I'm, well, I'm working in the center of it, linked in with top people all over the world. We talk a lot—and it's secured, our communications are closed. The real stuff we talk about we keep private among us—there's no way you could know what we talk about.
>
> "And we use that exact phrase—The Chaos. Those exact words. It's the same thing we all see coming.
>
> "But you couldn't know this. I'm blown away that you're saying this—that you're describing it the same way we do.
>
> "The exact same words. The Chaos."

Michael just looked back at the man and gave a little nod. The man held his eye and gave a small nod back. For that moment, they recognized each other, shared an understanding with an equality that was visible.

Then the man seemed to realize that there were other people around—that he, by definition, didn't talk about his work, much less the deeper realities of his international networks and their private convictions. He leaned back into his upright position, and with that move regained his professional demeanor.

I still didn't exist, nor did anyone in O'Hare's waiting lounge, except as backdrop. But Michael and the man continued to share an almost invisible smile.

I don't know if The Chaos is coming or not.

But in these conversations I realized that we—the global citizenry—need to start a more public, more informed conversation about the digital universe and all that it betokens for our future.

For this reason, the book is an anthropological *tour de horizon* exploring the unfolding digital universe as we live it: through the primary lens of in/security—political, economic, social, and personal. Or what Michael might call the innovation-power-chaos paradox.

And in/security, for me, is best explored through global digital outlaws and "the shadows."

LISA

WELCOME TO THE FUTURE. It all looks new—the shiny technology of today, sleeker and faster than ever before. It has changed the world, catalogued it carefully and stored it on the other side of a screen. It has, most definitely, changed the way we communicate. When else in history, after all, have we been able to talk directly to so many people so far away? However, as revolutionary as this Digital Revolution of ours may appear, much of the underlying concerns are the same as they have always been. Technology always brings new challenges, and we deal with those challenges in the same way we always have. Beneath the veneer of this brave new world is still the same basic human nature that has always been there.

We, the denizens of the digital age, are a step away from cyborg. Our technology has become nearly a part of us. To my generation, the Internet is not a place nor a separate realm but rather something that surrounds us like air.

It's overwhelming, almost infinite.

The impossible is almost nonexistent in this digital age. The present possibilities of the technologies are just beginning to be explored. As Scott Cook puts it, "We're still in the first minutes of the first day of the Internet revolution." There is still so much left uncharted.

Name something, and it can probably be done. Pacemaker—hacked. Bank account—robbed.

And the thing is, you can do it. You don't need connections. You don't need to be the Russian mob, though perhaps you are. You could be anyone. They could be anyone. It's all there for the taking, stored online. It's all invisible, it's all nothing more than data, but data can be everything—it can be billions of dollars, or the difference between your getting that job and someone else being hired. It can make or break politicians and teenage girls alike. It can bring down some of the United States' most expensive planes and take out nuclear factories.

I don't know the specifics, necessarily. I have seen only shadows of the dangers out there. Oh, I've heard stories of scams and phishing. I have neighbors to whom these things happen, these invasions of privacy, these stolen identities, these infestations. But me? I have nothing to hide, nothing to steal. I have the latest firewall, or perhaps a Mac, or the prudence and know-how to navigate the digital world safely.

And I, like so many others, repeat to myself a very old lie: I am safe. Because nothing has gone wrong before, it will not go wrong now. I've never bled, so I assume I'm invincible. Our familiarity with technology forms a false guarantee of security.

Yet we are not fools, and we know that, somewhere out there, there are "bad guys" who would do us wrong if allowed. We know that there are viruses that can ruin our computers, that there are predators searching for children, and that there are fewer Nigerian princes than the Internet would have us believe. We know that there are threats hidden in the hardware of our new technology, threats that the average computer user does not pretend to fully understand.

On some level, we are aware that we are exposed to a bevy of threats that we can essentially do nothing about. Technology surrounds us, just as ubiquitous as the air we breathe and, for many, almost as crucial. Without my laptop and smart phone, I know I wouldn't last a week at college. The busy professional might not make it even that long. We need technology, and yet we know it can fail us at any moment. Beyond just the fact that it can fail—batteries run out, and phones can break or get lost easily— there hides a more sinister threat, a threat we do not understand.

This book is an attempt to begin a discussion of this threat, with the hopes of making it more understandable and less taboo. In it, I try to step into the shadowy regions of my understanding of cyberspace, and explore the possibilities for both development and damage in the Digital Age. I take a look at what hacking is and is not, the obstacles in the way of an honest dialogue about cyberspace, the threats for the individual, the myths we create, and the way we interpret our personhood in the face of this brave new world. As Michael says, the Chaos is coming, and it's up to us to be ready for it when it arrives. In fact, it may already be here, with all its glorious complexity and grey area—this new realm of cyber-shadows.

Part One

Tour D'Horizon

New?

~ CN ~

"Ours is a real world. It is not for the faint of heart."

— Will Gragido and John Pirc[1]

"Albert Einstein said, 'I don't know what World War III will be fought with, but I do know the one after that will be fought with sticks and stones.'

"I also don't know what the next war will be like. But I do know the most dangerous will be those behind laptops.

"So much damage can be done by a gifted individual with a computer."

— Redshift[2]

It has been millennia since an individual had access to the resources to fight as an equal against an invading or ruling group. Once weapons, such as a sword, were cast of metal and required mining, forging, and skilled artisans—the average person could not compete against professional militaries. A lone individual could not mass an attack against Sumerian soldiers, invading Vikings, Crusaders, or WWII troops. That one sentence spans over five thousand years of examples.

This fact has given rise to empires, kingdoms, and the modern state. Until now.

For the first time in thousands of years, a civilian can stand equal to a ruling group or an invading hoard in critical ways. This one fact changes the very core of politics and power in the world. But how is as yet undetermined.

It is difficult to even imagine a social system where individuals can act with the autonomy and skill of nations. A thousand years ago it was inconceivable that a villager could amass the means to forge armor and weapons, buy and outfit horses, and meet an army head on.

In the last century the division between civilian and military has become far more stark: who among average townspeople can build an F-16 fighter plane, create a satellite-communications and espionage system, or acquire a nuclear submarine? Historically, individuals could challenge the political power of nation-states only when they formed into groups.

Computers and the Internet have changed all this.

"Power is being redefined," Jonathan Brossard, a leading cybersecurity researcher from France told me in an interview. Brossard had just presented his research (Black Hat 2012 conference) on hacking/flashing a computer's BIOS [basic input/output systems—initializes computer and loads operating system] *before* the device was bought (anywhere in the supply chain)—thus maintaining core control of the machine no matter what security measures a user employed. Remarkably, his exploit was effective for over 230 different motherboards in various computers.

> It is possible to conceive of circumstances where a person can stand on a more equal footing, make a successful challenge to a state. Skills are normally linear; and now in the world today people who are massively skilled at digital technologies can achieve a lot more than an entire population—even those counting in the millions.

Take Charlie Miller. When he breaks an iPhone every year he is doing better at security than entire organizations like Apple—and Apple is wealthy and powerful enough to compete with nation-states.[3]

The production, distribution, and availability of resources—hardware and software alike—provides part of the explanation for such radical transformations. Computing hardware is mass produced worldwide. No core section of this is classified and unavailable to the average buyer. Software—even at the most sophisticated levels—is written equally by private citizens and military specialists.

No operating system is built entirely from scratch anymore: at the most basic level this involves the creation of millions of lines of code that must be tested for countless thousands of serious bugs and vulnerabilities. The same is true for the core programs that run everything from Internet browsers to data processing. People buy Windows or Mac operating systems or download Linux, load browsers to access the Internet, upload communications and file transfer software, and use image-recognition packages.

No country has a secured industry manufacturing every component essential to computers: the motherboard components, wireless cards, hard drives, network-cabling, jump drives, ad infinitum.

Top military elite and the unknown citizen all buy essential hardware and use core software from the same places. This is openly acknowledged at the leading hacker/security conferences attended by government and civilian expert alike. Shawn Henry, former head of the FBI's cyber-intelligence, noted in his 2012 Black Hat plenary talk:

Cyber is the great equalizer. A $500 laptop and an internet connection, and anyone from anywhere in the world can attack governments and industries—in their pajamas sitting in their living room. 2.3 billion have net connections last time I checked.

Computer threat is the most significant threat we face as a society—not just as a country, but as a society in the world.

In terms of cybercrime alone, General Keith Alexander, the current director of the National Security Agency (NSA) and the commander of USCYBERCOM, has called it "the greatest transfer of wealth in history:"[4]

> And that's our future disappearing in front of us. So, let me put this in context, if I could. We have this tremendous opportunity with the devices that we use. We're going mobile, but they're not secure. Tremendous vulnerabilities. Our companies use these, our kids use these, we use these devices, and they're not secure.[5]

Since the genius behind breakthroughs in computing are as likely to come from a teenager coding in their basement or a private security specialist as it is from national military and intelligence, no one at these conferences perpetuates the illusion that super-power governments are qualitatively ahead of civilians in computer knowledge and power.[6]

These facts are not secret. They circulate among security professionals, across hacker websites, through cyber-elite conferences to bubble up periodically in mainstream newspapers and magazines, TV shows and movies.

Discussions about solutions are emerging across the world. They are as new and as fragile as the digital realities they address. Agreements and antipathies abound. Perhaps one of the only things most cyber-literati agree on is that crafting solutions based on "today"—on what has been and not on what is developing—has been a sure means to disaster for millennia. As Redshift told me in conversation at Black Hat 2012:

> Some attacks out there are so sophisticated that our minds want to deny the possibility of this happening.
>
> People have to realize there are people out there smarter than them, and just because you are a hot button today, there are smarter people out there. The greatest hackers out there are the ones we never hear about.

We can model and "do scenarios" and all other manner of security prediction analyses, but these address what we know.

I am worried about the unseen variables—the uncalculated, unaccounted for variables. Sometimes these can turn out to be minor. But they may be the ones that shift things fundamentally in the world.

I generally find two main reactions to "cyber-threats": people who see how available cyber-technology can be used to undermine the core institutions of countries and could conceivably cause a nation-state collapse; and those who think these fears are overinflated and don't really see the serious threat of stealing millions of credit cards, bank account information, or Facebook posts.

Redshift's quote raises a third way of responding to threats of cyber-insecurity—beyond seeing either the logic, or the impossibility, of widespread danger and potential collapse. It is a view shared as well at a national level by such leaders as Toomas Hendrik Ilves, the President of Estonia. Knowledge, the imagination to create and confront the new and unknown, and responsible citizenry define the core of this approach. As Ilves writes:

> Notions of a nation's size, wealth, power, military might, population and G.D.P. mean something altogether different from what they meant a generation ago.
>
> These relations are in constant flux, and old assumptions no longer hold. Today, a small, poor East European country can be a world leader in e-governance and cyber-security...
>
> In a modern digitalized world it is possible to paralyze a country without attacking its defense forces: The country can be ruined by simply bringing its SCADA systems to a halt. [SCADA—Supervisory Control and Data Acquisition, generally refers to Industrial Control Systems: computer systems that control industrial, (critical) infrastructure and facility-processes from airports and ships to space stations.] To impoverish a country one can erase its banking records. The most sophisticated military technology can be rendered irrelevant. In cyberspace, no country is an island.
>
> This requires rethinking some of our core philosophical notions of

modern society: the relations between the public and private spheres, between privacy and identity.[7]

Estonia is one of the most cyber-advanced nations today. While many in the world may stumble over the definition of SCADA systems or the ability to creatively theorize privacy and identity at a national level, most Estonians don't. As one Estonian hacker told me with a hint of pride: "We believe coding and programming should be taught to all children in grade school. This way, people—citizens—know; we lead solutions, rather than being controlled by them."

New eras, emergent frontiers, cannot be fully understood through the lens of what is known and what has been. We need to turn our analyses to the unknown and the emergent—the horizon beckoning at the edges of our imaginations.

Endnotes

[1] Will Gragido, John Pirc, *Cybercrime and Espionage*, 2011:179.

[2] Redshift, personal communication, Black Hat Conference, Las Vegas, 2012.

[3] Interview at Black Hat Conference, Las Vegas, 7/28/2012.

[4] DefCon 20 Conference Keynote speech, Las Vegas, July 2012; American Enterprise Institute event "Cybersecurity and American Power."

[5] While cybercrime statistics are difficult to verify, and a great deal of controversy and disagreement marks the topic, at the time of General Alexander's talk in 2012:

> Symantec placed the cost of IP theft to the United States companies at $250 billion a year, global cybercrime at $114 billion annually ($388 billion when you factor in downtime), and McAfee estimates that $1 trillion was spent globally under remediation.

Discussed in Pierluigi Paganini, "Ponemon Statistics on Cost of Cybercrime for 2012," *Infosec Island,* October 10, 2012, *http://www.infosecisland.com/blogview/22541-Ponemon-Statistics-on-Cost-of-Cybercrime-for-2012.html.* Accessed 11/03/2012.

[6] Toby Sacker (National Security Agency's "Information Assurance and Security Testing") said in the Black Hat conference keynote panel "Past -> Future (8/5/2011):"

> In the cyber realm, the good and the bad all use the same technology. All of the government is hopelessly dependent on commercial vendors, manufacturers, supplies—the same ones available to anybody, everybody.
>
> The world is far more interconnected. We can't secure the DOD and make it better without everyone getting better. Including the bad guys. Having standards and security in government will be built on

the same technology as the bad guys have. There is no more neutral ground—no DOD place with different technology than is available in the world in general.

[7] Toomas Hendrik Ilves, "Cybersecurity: A View from the Front," The *New York Times*, April 11, 2013, *http://www.nytimes.com/2013/04/12/opinion/global/cybersecurity-a-view-from-the-front.html?* Accessed 4/15/2013.

– Tour D'Horizon –
Anthropology in the Digital World
~ CN ~

"A few decades ago, some genius had this outrageous idea: 'Let's put everything online.' Everything. Measureless reams of information all piled up on the World Wide Web.

"The audacity of this concept should not go unappreciated."

– Derek Slater[1]

For an anthropologist, "cyber" isn't a dry designation.[2] It can't be comprehended solely through parts or processes or particulars alone. Hundreds of millions of people today are variously interacting to produce computer components, software, net-cultures, laws, and communication systems. Their values shape how they "make" the cyber-universe, including its "shadows."

Something illuminates the heartbeat of humanity; something gives meaning to action that is shared among people. For us, both external and internal landscapes—the material and the intangible—are equally important and richly evocative.

Anthropologically, it is not enough to say that "15% of all

computers are infected with malware that turns them into zombies in a botnet controlled by bot-masters." Nor is it really enough to say that this enables them to steal all the information on the infected computers—for political gain, economic crime, or social harm.

It's the "why?" What goals are driving actions? Not just personal goals of profit or control, but larger global ones defining the most fundamental realities of power, politics, economics, and identity in the unfolding world.

"If I gave you a piece of paper and asked you to draw a picture of the Internet, what would you do? Many older people would draw a computer. But a computer is the tool used to access the Internet, not the Internet itself. Many of you would draw a network of lines crisscrossing the world. Closer, I would say but how does that differ from a depiction of phone lines?

"A very few of you, the most clever, would say that I might as well be asking you to draw what it means to be American. The Internet consists of people, but not their physical presence. More accurately, it is people's Minds which inhabit the Internet. These Minds are what wander websites, leave tracks in the form of comments and page views, and ultimately create the world they inhabit. It is possible to give examples of the Internet's effects, to draw symbols, but impossible to draw the thing itself."

– Mark Stechschulte[3]

The Internet, as it weaves across billions of computers, smartphones, and routing systems, is a vast, sprawling, constantly-changing and emerging cyberscape. It is, as well, something of an un-mapable map.

It is like, metaphorically, millions of people bringing their own ideas of what Lego building blocks are and creating their own little addition to everyone else's Lego constructions—all linking up into an enormous reticulated Lego empire so massive and complex that no one individual can see its entirety.

Oftentimes the ideas people have of the Internet are laden with myths, emotions, politics, and worldviews. Tom Boellstorff captures this well:

> Too often, virtual worlds are described in terms of breathless futurism and capitalist hype. Above all they seem *new*, and this apparent newness is central to their being interpreted as harbingers of a coming utopia of unforeseen possibilities, intimations of a looming dystopia of alienation, or trinkets of a passing fad.[4]

We are still in the infancy of the Internet era where maps have the equivalent of those in the Middle Ages on which large swaths are marked "Dragons Be Here," landmasses are dotted with notations like "unreliable information," and ocean soundings shift from numbers of fathoms to the mere words "very deep" and "unknown."

Briefest of Overviews

"Knowledge is power -> Information is power -> All your info is owned by [malware] Flame."

– anonymous post[5]

THE INTERNET

Google brings us the world we can see—that is to say, the visible net-world that can be reached through public search engines. If the parable of the anthropological village is used, the public Internet is the town square—pleasant open spaces where you can see all the shops and buildings open to you, and where buses take you on journeys along clearly marked routes. But this is only a small part of the cyber-world.

Public search engines like Google generally don't reach the

"invisible net"—what is often called the darknet or deepnet. If you were to stand in the town square looking out across the village-scape, the deepnet lies beyond your vision. It is the locked doors on shops, the speak-easies that require passwords to gain entry, and the neighborhoods where the city buses don't run; the high-security, high-tech repositories, the back alleys, safe houses, and secret "no-fly zones"; the gambling parlors, brothels, and opium dens; the libraries and research archives; the barrios not marked on the maps. It is the meeting places of poets, dissidents, cat lovers, scientists, criminals, and dreamers.

This analogy works on a second level as well. As with land-scapes, the invisible net is not structurally different or apart from the surface net. It is merely a locked gate to a dwelling, a trail to a neighborhood that you won't find without a guide, special trans-port, or certain language skills.

No one claims to have a precise figure for the size of the invis-ible net. Most agree that it is some 500 times the size of the surface Google-accessible net.[6]

The darknet is made up of roiling contradictions and myriad actors. It is the sanctuary of people seeking a voice under repressive governments, the haunt of criminals, the fox-holes of cyber-soldiers, the library of the latest scientific advancements, and the living room of file-sharers swapping media, music, and camaraderie. It is the protectorate of Internet-creators and supporters dedicated to freedom of communication.

The Internet connects everything that has a computing device wishing to communicate with other computing devices: comput-ers, smartphones, electrical grids, security systems, pacemakers, smart-home controls, jet consoles, financial wire-transfer systems, televisions, satellites in space, laser surgery, wireless toys and baby monitors, navigational and guidance devices, automobiles, E-ZPass transponders for toll roads, security systems, ebooks, and cloud storage systems.

Copper wire, fiber optic cable, and radio waves are the transport systems of the Internet. Electricity, sound waves, and light particles carry bundles of data that translate into 0s and 1s; these then translate into the programs, pictures, words, sounds, and social life of the net.

Malware hitches rides in the software and along these transport systems of the Internet—carried as code along cables and radio waves in a picture shared with a friend, an infected jump drive, or a mean version of Java you use to check the weather. It would seem all societies are plagued with disease-carrying viruses and pathogens.

ECOSYSTEMS AND THEIR VULNERABILITIES

"Until 1992, it was against the law to use the Internet for commercial purposes…that means that 20 years ago, nobody was doing anything commercial on the Internet. Ten years ago, what were you doing on the Internet, Dana? Buying a book for the first time or something like that?

"In the intervening decade, we've turned this sort of Swiss cheese, cool network, which has brought us dramatic productivity and all and pleasure into the backbone of virtually everything we do.

"International finance, personal finance, command and control of military, manufacturing controls, the controls in our critical infrastructure, all of our communications, virtually all of our activities are either on the Internet or exposed to the Internet. And it's the same Internet that was Swiss cheese 20 years ago and it's Swiss cheese now.

"So this gives a natural and profound advantage to attack on this network over defense. That's why we're in the predicament we're in."

– Joel Brenner [7]

"Ecosystem" is one of the more commonly used words describing the digital-world. In one sense, this is a somewhat misleading term. Nature enjoys remarkable diversity.

Not so with the computer realm.

A few core operating systems exist. A limited range of largely standardized programs animate the daily life of computers and their net-connections. Howard Shrobe, MIT computer scientist and DARPA [Defense Advanced Research Projects Agency] program manager, says this monoculture is one of the biggest challenges facing computing today:

> Nature abhors monocultures, and that's exactly what we have in the computer world today...Eighty percent are running the same operating system.[8]

The Windows/Linux/Mac architectures, Internet browsers like Firefox and Safari, communication and authentication software allowing the net to function, JavaScript, Adobe, PDF, jump drives, wireless and Bluetooth technologies, multimedia programs, encryption and anti-virus software, ad infinitum are pervasive across a wide swath of the world's computers.

No one, including governments today, can custom-create and build all necessary components for entire computer networks to ensure security—some systems, yes; but not all. Even the most secured systems rely on at least some hardware and software bought from global vendors.

The fundamental architecture of computing was created to be an "open" (versus a secure) communications system. Hundreds of millions upon billions of lines of code housed in minerals, metal, plastic, and glass *are* the computer-net. It is a proverbial vast dwelling with myriad open windows, unlocked doors, faulty alarms, and uncharted passageways.

Countless numbers of hackers have spent untold time since the inception of computers cracking these codes to gain entry. People share the information of their exploits, and e-libraries emerged.

Today, anyone with computer access can find information on how to gain unauthorized entry into just about any core computer-net program/technology.

NETIZENS

"The concept of a 'person' as the only threat has lost its meaning. It may be a server; we can be at war with a network."
— *David Goldman*[9]

When a new technology emerges in the world, the scramble to control it can be life and death. Even grade-schoolers know empires rise and fall on innovations in technology and the ability to harness these for one's own group and against others.

The majority of cyber-literati, as far as I can tell, do not dabble in geopolitics. They are not seeking political power or economic hegemony. They are technical and technological artists—some brilliant. Their glory comes from creating elegant systems of code. Whatever goal variously drives them, they are the ones capable of creating, fashioning, and maintaining the core technologies of the emergent digital empire; outcome as yet unknown.

The political leaders, the CEOs of industry, and the military generals know the new era depends on this technology—technology for the most part they themselves are incapable of making.

> Do not be deceived by uniforms, theirs or ours, or language that serves as uniforms, or behaviors. There is no theirs or ours, no us or them. There are only moments of awareness at the nexus where fiction myth and fact touch, there are only moments of convergence. But if it is all on behalf of the Truth it is Hacking.[10]

This is a new wild card in the power equation. One person can hack the government's secrets, interrupt financial systems, ransom energy grids, create new sat-linked communication relays.

Technical experts are not restricted to the political and industrial elite. They are the proverbial anyone.

The architects of the net—the people who know the digital back alleys and the passwords for the cyber speak-easies—do not follow neat social categories.

In fact, they violate the rules of social logic the nation-state world has come to embrace. Rules about the forging of national identities; the divisions between legal and illegal; the ways people do and do not interact; the distinctions among war, crime, profit, and the meaning of power. Values about who associates with whom. Following are a few examples:

• Hackers living in their parent's basement creating exploits showing the vulnerabilities of large corporations (probably called criminal hacking by the public media) are as likely to then build the patches to fix them, while sharing ideas with the FBI or a hacker-genius in the Naval cyber-intelligence unit.

• A cyber-expert from Verizon or DARPA hangs out with hacker-kids at a conference swapping the latest breakthroughs and looking for the emergent.

• A security guru in America is online with peers in China, Estonia, Brazil, and Vanatu working on reverse-engineering a new variant of botnet code.

• High school students are trying to figure out answers to cyber-crackdowns in repressive regimes half a world away, feeling closer to the downtrodden they only know by words on a screen than they do to the teachers in front of them handing out words on a page.

- Social-bots—automated computer programs passing themselves off as real people—chat with Facebook friends who think they're befriending humans.

The hacker community understandably bonds together. It is not then surprising that in the USA a teenage hacker, a jean-clad security expert, and a cyber-weapons scientist in the military would put their heads together over a particularly difficult new technological development.

No doctor can operate without vast libraries and good teachers backing their training; no economist or physicist can create an entire mathematical system to calculate the equations necessary for solving pressing problems.

The Net is new and, for now, the digital-hacker-experts are the libraries, the compendium of teachers, and the cohort forging the foundational equations.

THE PLAYERS AND THE SHADOWS

"Our entire world is being controlled and operated by tiny invisible 1s and 0s that are flashing through the air and flashing through the wires around us. So if that's what controls our world, ask yourself who controls the 1s and 0s? It's the geeks and computer hackers of the world."
— *Christopher "Commander X" Doyon*[11]

There is a stark class system in the computer world. It divides not by money or traditional power, but by knowledge.

> Geniuses build elegant code-scapes—programs. Others find tiny fissures in these code-scapes, a command miswritten or forgotten, and build elegant exploits—malware.

> The classical individual hacker sees exploits like "counting coup"—not for profit but for the recognition of being a cyber-literati. Some work for business, while others work for academia, and still others for government—helping to develop security.

> Hacktivists, groups like Anonymous, aren't anonymous to the public—in a curious blend of social justice, illicit interests, rebel morals, and counting coup, they tend to take credit for their exploits. On a deeper level, as Gabriella Coleman writes:

> Anonymous' activities, however disparate and paradoxical on their surface, have tapped into a deep disenchantment with the political status quo, without positing a utopian vision—or any overarching agenda—in response.

To Coleman, though Anonymous may variously be irreverent, activist, and at times vindictive or disdainful of the law, they also represent what Ernst Bloch calls "the principle of hope."[12]

> Transnational criminal enterprises (TCE) don't take such credit. As leading cryptologist Bruce Schneier cautions:

> Cyberspace threats are real. Military threats might get the publicity, but the criminal threats are both more dangerous and more damaging.[13]

Their strength at present comes in their ability to fly under the radar, and in the fact that most of JQPublic don't really know what they do. These are not weak connections of credit-card thieves, but complex and sophisticated international business-model organizations capable of controlling significant global wealth.

> Government bodies know that sovereign power is now being determined in part within a cyber-universe that has little respect for borders and boundaries. Schneier continues:

> We're starting to see a power grab in cyberspace by the world's militaries: large-scale monitoring of networks, military control of internet standards, even military takeover of cyberspace...countries are engaging in offensive actions in cyberspace, with tools like Stuxnet and Flame.[14]

Most now accept WW3 (World War III)—or as some see it WW 3.0 (Web War 3.0)—will include cyber-components. No one agrees on how many or how much. WW 1.0, the first web war, is generally considered the cyber-attack on Estonia in 2007; and the second the Stuxnet attack on Iranian nuclear facilities in 2010-2011.

> In a hazy realm somewhere between FUD (fear, uncertainty, doubt—a classic cyber-analysis) and reality rest a host of possible actors operating outside (and potentially against) the sovereign state: terrorists, rogue powers, and, to quote Michael Gross, "virtual insurgents" and "guerrilla hackers."[15] Zheng Bu et. al. see a more organized emergence of cyber-armies throughout the world:

> Some hacktivists will operate along the same lines as the various "cyberarmies" that primarily flourish in nondemocratic or nonsecular states (Iranian Cyber Army, Pakistan Cyber Army, ChinaHonker group, etc.). Mostly used for defacement in the past two years, the armies will move to more disruptive actions in the new year.[16]

> In this flux of identities, many recognize "the undefined" and the emergent. The lines between Transnational Criminal Enterprises (TCEs), espionage, government, military, and business are deeply blurred. Stealing data, industrial secrets, and monies can turn a profit, but can also undermine the integrity of a country's core institutions to a degree that could be deemed an act of war. As siavash explains, quoting a former Secretary of Defense:

> Leon Panetta, the US secretary of defense, said this January that "the reality is that there is the cyber capacity to basically bring down our power grid…to paralyze our financial system in this country to virtually paralyze our country."[17]

> The lines between human and techne, to use Boellstorff's[18] term, are becoming equally blurred. Enter "SocialBots," "Chat-Bots," or just Bots for short.

SocialBots are automated programs—chains of code that roam social media introducing themselves to humans *as* humans and variously extracting information, infiltrating people's lives and devices, working to manipulate social behavior, and seeking to become "cultural tipping points." It is becoming increasingly common to share the adventures of your day with a Facebook Friend or act on info re-Tweeting virally without realizing your friend Pat is a bot.

The Internet is a hotbed of bots, variously programmed by governments (ours and theirs), militaries, industries, criminal enterprises, spies, pranksters, and influence-peddlers to chat amiably while scoping you and scooping your data.

For the annual Loebner Prize, both humans and artificial intelligence programs passing themselves off as humans are presented to a panel of judges to see if the experts can identify which are the "non-humans." The contest is based on Alan Turing's classic thought-experiment at the dawn of computing: if a computer can pass itself off as human to impartial judges, it could be seen as "thinking." In 2008 the top chatbot fooled 25% of the 12 judges. The co-founder of the Loebner Prize, psychologist Robert Epstein, admits he was duped for four months by a chatbot he met online.[19]

THE SHADOWS AND THE PLAYERS, *WRIT LARGE*

The "players" introduced above—if considering the cyber-shadows in any way—are the ones that emerge from immersion in cyber-literature, hacking discussions, and digital-research largely in the English-speaking arenas.

I originally met the "global cyber-shadows" in a far different way—one that is seldom easily visible in the arenas discussed above. But the "shadow-players," as I got to know them, are perhaps a core backbone of the emerging digital world as we really live it.

Curiously, at the time, these people did not stand out as "hackers," as "cyber-literati," as the creators of a new world. They populate my publications like anyone else. At the time I was writing a lot about how very poor people who had suffered devastating wars throughout the world showed remarkable creativity in building viable economic and survival infrastructures from ashes.

Over the last fifteen years, I have written of people like:

- Wink and Tiago who had state-of-the-art globally linked computer communications systems with their own generators in small mud and cement back rooms in remote African towns;[20]
- barefoot teenage soldiers sitting on tree stumps in the forests of impoverished global warzones wearing only tattered shorts and a T-shirt, AK-47 leaning up against the stump, working at sat-linked laptops;[21] and
- the businessmen in Sri Lanka who explained to me how to hack into satellite communications.[22]

Wink lives in a dusty one-road border town, trading with itinerant truckers who ply the most war-torn and remote regions, and who often carry millions of dollars' worth of cargo per load.

Tiago made enough money brokering essential supplies in warzones to send his son to an elite European university to learn computer science. He could reach his son in Europe on speed dial from Africa even when his computers crashed and the region's electricity failed, and his son would walk him through re-set. I was sitting with him having a coffee in his remote village in Southern Africa when a truck in a cross-border cargo run in a war-afflicted area disappeared and his computer system blue-screened. He whipped out his sat-linked cell, called his son in Oxford, and quickly followed his son's instructions to get the system back up and tracking the truck-run (which was avoiding border guards and customs). Cows munched grass in the dirt road outside, the town's small electrical grid was down, people walked by carrying water home from town spigots because they lacked plumbing. Tiago had his system up before I finished my coffee. The year was 2001.

The child-soldiers explored chat rooms with technical advice and top blockbuster movie releases worldwide—a global-generation educating themselves. In 2002 I watched hit US movies like this and emailed friends on rogue and jerry-rigged internet connections that I had seen them before they did in urban USA. At the time this country was listed as the poorest in the world by global economic indices.

The Sri Lankan helped develop his country's infrastructure in ways that surpassed the stunted policies allowed by the warring political parties. In the aftermath of the Tsunami's destruction in 2005, these kinds of communications systems were life-saving. I returned to the USA assuming everyone knew about things like hacking into satellite communications—it was such obvious knowledge here.

I also assumed that the first generation smart phone I had picked up on the streets of Singapore in 2004—and had configured for global net access by a fourteen-year-old boy selling sim cards in Sri Lanka—would be easy for my USA cell company to configure when I got home. Two years and about a dozen top-level cell company tech experts later, my cell never could get full or accurate net access, and I gave it up for the first smart phone available in the USA.

There are millions of Winks and Tiagos, kid-geniuses, and smart businesspeople all adding a piece—some within the confines of the nation-state and its initiatives, some in new and creative ways.

CYBER-NINJA

> *"Stealthy reconnaissance is the ninja's chief contribution to victory. The ninja should move undetected into the enemy's area of influence and gather pertinent information about the enemy's strengths and weaknesses. Escaping in a manner that prevents his presence from ever being known, the ninja then returns to his allies with the knowledge that will permit an attack at the most opportune time and place, leaving the enemy bewildered by the fact that the attack 'just happened' to befall them at their weakest point."*
>
> *– Toshitsugu Takamatsu, the 33rd grand master of Togakure-ryū*[23]

There is the almost universal agreement among computing security experts that intruders have the upper hand at present—whether the latter are nation-states, criminal organizations, or lone actors.

> [T]he gulf between the mindset of the attackers and the mindset of the victims symbiotically creates a perfect storm, which is peculiar to this specific moment in history.[24]

In considering this, many security experts quote leading historical military and political philosophers dating back several thousand years—Sun Tzu and *The Art of War*, the Romans Seneca and Cicero, and more recently Miyamoto's *Book of Five Rings* on samurai military strategy, and enduring stories of the ninja.

As Gragido and Pirc explain it, "what's old is new again." Humans, they say, have been creating and subverting laws and governance for more than 10,000 years. As ideologies and technologies evolve, so too have notions of good and evil, and one way of life replaces another over and again.

Few quote the mostly western politico-military theorists omnipresent in most of today's academic and media discussions of security, from von Clausewitz to Churchill. Those I encounter who do quote von Clausewitz hold that real change is not imminent; that the conventional rules of crime, war, and conquest will continue to predominate; and that no matter what people and technologies may emerge, the force of the nation-state and its militaries will prevail.

Echoing the sentiments of numerous cyber-analysts, Gragido and Pirc caution:

> In *The Art of War*, Sun Tzu wrote, "If you know the enemy and know yourself, you need not fear the result of a hundred battles. If you know yourself but not the enemy, for every victory gained you will also suffer a defeat. If you know neither the enemy nor yourself, you will succumb in every battle." From the writing and wisdom of Sun Tzu we learn that without a complete and comprehensive knowledge of ourselves and our adversaries, we cannot hope to arrive at a position of victor. This is critical whether on the conventional battlefield, in the cyber realm, or in intelligence analysis environments.[25]

Sun Tzu and ninja-hackers also provide a platform for people to grapple with the deeper moral issues of cyber-life. In their book *Ninja Hacking* Wilhelm and Andress point out that classic Japanese Ninjutsu texts portray ninjas as motivated by universal justice and a peaceful balance in society. Quoting Toshitsugu Takamatsu, the 33rd grand master of Togakure-ryū, they say the ethics of ninja historically and today are similar: "Family, community, homeland, and 'appropriateness' determine when a ninja should act, not power, money, political obligation, or thrill of violence and adventure."[26]

Though they themselves seldom say this explicitly, in the final summation I see cyber philosopher-analysts trying to convey some essence of emergent forms of power as yet unknown, and to grapple with social and personal roles that defy the boundaries and definitions we have come to hold as normal and enduring.

Endnotes

[1] Derek Slater, "Tangled Web: Facebook, SEO, and Black-hat Tactics Colliding (Still)" March 15, 2012, *http://www.csoonline.com/article/print/702253*. Accessed 4/07/2012.

[2] For overview examples, see: Gabriella Coleman, "Ethnographic Approaches to Digital Media," *Annual Review of Anthropology* 39: 487-505, 2010; Tom Boellstroff, Bonnie, Nardi, Celia Pearce and T. L. Taylor, *Ethnography and Virtual Worlds: A Handbook of Method*, Princeton: Princeton University Press, 2012; Daniel Miller and Heather Horst (eds.), *Digital Anthropology*, Bloomsbury Academic, 2012; Andrew Feenberg and Norm Friesen (eds.), *(Re)Inventing the Internet: Critical Case Studies*, Rotterdam: Sense Publishers, 2012.

[3] Mark Stechschulte, "*The Internet Nation*," February 12, 2012, *http://blogs.nd.edu/totheinternetandbeyond/2012/02/21/internet_natio/*. Accessed 3/20/2012.

[4] Tom Boellstorff, *Coming of Age in Second Life: An Anthropologist Explores the Virtually Human*, Princeton: Princeton University Press, 2010:32.

[5] Anonymous post, 6/4/2012:10:24pm, *http://threatpost.com/en_us/blogs/flame-malware-raises-need-open-talk-use-cyberweapons-060112*.

[6] Michael Bergman, "The Deep Web: Surfacing Hidden Value," *The Journal of Electronic Publishing* 7(1), 2001.

[7] Joel Brenner, quoted in: Dana Gardner, "Corporate data, supply chains remain vulnerable to cyber crime attacks," Interarbor Solutions, June 5, 2012, *http://www.it-director.com/technology/security/content.php?ci*. Accessed 6/28/2012.

[8] John Markoff, "Killing the Computer to Save It," *The New York Times*, October 29, 2012, *http://www.nytimes.com/2012/10/30/science/rethinking-the-computer-at-80.html*. Accessed 11/2/12.

[9] David Goldman, "Government Hackers," *Money,* July 28, 2011, *http://www.money.com/2011/07/28/technology/government_hackers/index.htm?iid=EAL.*

[10] Richard Thieme, "Hacker Generations," February 5, 2009, *http://www.thiemeworks.com/hacker-generations/.* Accessed 1/1/2013.

[11] Quote by Christopher "Commander X" Doyon, facing 15 years in jail for hactivism exploits with a group associated with Anonymous; quoted in: Pierluigi Paganini, "Has Anonymous Infiltrated the US Government?" *Infosec Island,* May 16, 2012, *http://www.infosecisland.com/blogview/21339-Has-Anonymous-Infiltrated-the-US-Government.html.* Accessed 6/4/2012.

[12] Gabriella Coleman, "Our Weirdness Is Free, The Logic of Anonymous—Online army, agent of chaos, and seeker of justice," *Triple Canopy,* January 2012, *http://canopycanopycanopy.com/issues/15/contents/our_weirdness_is_free.* Accessed 5/10/13. See also: Gabriella Coleman, *Coding Freedom: The Ethics and Aesthetics of Hacking,* Princeton: Princeton University Press, 2012.

[13] Bruce Schneier, "An International Cyberwar Treaty Is the Only Way to Stem the Threat," *U.S. News Weekly,* June 8, 2012, *http://www.usnews.com/debate-club.*

[14] ibid.

[15] Michael Joseph Gross, "World War 3.0," *Vanity Fair,* May 2012, *http://www.vanityfair.com/culture/2012/05/internet-regulation-war-sopa-pipa-defcon-hacking.*

[16] Zheng Bu et. al., "McAfee: 2012 Threat Predictions," Santa Clara, CA: McAfee Labs.

[17] Katia Moskvitch, "The world's five biggest cyber threats," April 25, 2012, *http://www.bbc.co.uk/news/technology-17846185.*

[18] Boellstorff, op. cit.

[19] Brian Christian, "Rise of the Chatbots," *Smithsonian*.com, July/August 2012.

[20] Carolyn Nordstrom, *Global Outlaws: Crime, Money, and Power in the Contemporary World,* Berkeley: University of California Press, 2007.

[21] Carolyn Nordstrom, *Shadows of War: Violence, Power, and International Profiteering in the 21st Century,* Berkeley: University of California Press, 2004; and *A Different Kind of War Story,* Philadelphia: University of Pennsylvania Press, 1997.

[22] Carolyn Nordstrom, "IT and the Illicit," In: *Bombs and Bandwidth: The Emerging Relationship Between Information Technology and Security,* Robert Latham (ed.) & Social Science Research Council, New York: The New Press, 2003:235-250.

[23] Quoted in: Thomas Wilhelm and Jason Andress, *Ninja Hacking*, Boston: Elsevier, 2011:38.

[24] Will Gragido, Daniel Molina, John Pirc and Nick Selby, *Blackhatonomics: An Inside Look at the Economics of Cybercrime*, Waltham, MA: Elsevier Press, 2013:1.

[25] Will Gragido and John Pirc, *Cybercrime and Espionage*, Boston: Elsevier, 2011:229.

[26] Wilhelm and Andress, op. cit., 19.

LIFE IN THE DIGITAL VILLAGE

~ LC ~

I FIND MYSELF LIVING online as much, if not sometimes even more, as I do offline.

I am glued to Google. I use it as my second brain. It knows the lyrics to my favorite song better than I do, and can find the name of that one guy from that one thing. My phone is constantly at my side, with all the information I could imagine. All of my friends and I are comfortable and familiar with the technologies of today. We have built our lives around them, and even in them, with a substantial part of our social lives playing out online. Just as there are banks and movie theaters and shops and everything in the real world, you have that online too; and around these things little pockets of community form. People are living decent chunks of their lives online. You have a lit area where you go, where your friends go. For me, it's about ten websites—Google, my top five favorite comedy websites, my email, and a handful of writing sites. I would get swept up in the Internet—I would be in line for Block-buster and I'd be posting on my phone to this writing forum that I was honestly obsessed with, and the people on it—we'd never met—but they were my friends. I wished them happy birthday, I talked to them almost every day, and when I stopped going on the site, it felt like a graduation, and I look back nostalgically on it. I miss it, and I miss these people—these people that I have never met and will never meet in real life.

If I were to tell you my online handle, you could watch me grow up. You could find my neglected NeoPets account, visit my Polyvore page and see my sets evolve, and watch my Tetris skills improve. You could construct a very comprehensive collage of me, at every stage of my life. I've spent massive amounts of time on the Internet, and yet I know very little about it.

Familiarity and understanding do not go hand in hand. I am very familiar with the technology, but I don't understand it. To me, it all seems like magic. I talk to my phone, and it figures out what I'm saying. I play a snippet of a song to Shazam, and it finds the name and artist of the tune. It seems like a cool magic trick. I don't know how it's possible, but it doesn't surprise me that it is—I assume it is possible. I assume that anything is possible. The cyber world is exempt from the laws of physics, and so I do not even have that baseline to operate from. I know a few basic concepts, but the bulk of it is mysterious. I have seen only the shadowy outline of these cyber threats. I know they are there, but they feel more like folklore than actuality.

And so, when faced with things we do not understand, we react the same way we always have. We create a mythology, a symbolic shorthand to help name the shadows, to make them seem a little less unknown. A set of rules that borders on superstitious governs the way we use and discuss the Internet. Like the Sumerians giving stories to the skies, we create a codex to help chart the vast cyber realm.

These rules are not all bad. Don't open SPAM. Don't download free stuff. Don't visit shady websites. Conventional wisdom is just as valuable in the cyber world as it is in the real world. The idea, however, that these rules are comprehensive is ludicrous.

In many ways, our digital mythology is doing its job. It allows people to play the odds without realizing they are gambling. Statistically speaking, it is unlikely that technology will crumble around you tomorrow. It will likely strike some stranger, however. The myths allow us to continue living our lives feeling as though we're in control of outcomes. They "ritualize man's optimism...enhance his faith in the victory of hope over fear" and "express the greater value for man of confidence over doubt, of steadfastness over vacillation, of optimism over pessimism." (Malinowski, Magic, Science and Religion). This is crucial. It prevents widespread panic, and allows the machine of the everyday to roll on unimpeded.

In other ways, this myth is harmful. Myths create taboos and silent spaces in culture. A reticence about reality develops as a sort of coping mechanism. Even though the threat of hacking is very real, you feel like you're wearing tin foil on your head as soon as you start talking about it. Being afraid of technology seems ludicrous. "Cybercrime" sounds like a catchphrase for local channels on slow news days, not something that the educated Internet user worries about. Viruses are viewed almost like STDs—the only people who get them are dirty porn aficionados and foolish first-time browsers who are naively seduced by clearly dangerous things. Identity theft is for the uninitiated. Online stalking is a concern only to people foolish enough to put personal information in public places. Because our myths eliminate the idea that venturing online is a gambling game, we tend to blame the victims. Incidents are seen as preventable. Don't walk down dark alleys alone at night if you don't want to be mugged; don't venture into the dark places of the Internet if you don't want viruses or worse. However, many of the threats are very real, and we have no mechanism to deal with them yet.

The unknown seems omnipotent. Because I do not quite understand the rules of the Internet, I don't know what the limitations are. I know the limits of crime in the kinetic world. I know that someone needs to have a gun if they want to shoot me, I know someone needs to be nearby to pick my pocket, and I know that all actions are governed by a set of physical laws. Online, however, that all changes. I have no idea what is and isn't possible. I think that I'm Internet savvy, but if you were to ask me what a hacker can do, the truth is that I can't tell you what they can't do. Because digital technology is outside of my current understanding, I do not know its parameters. If my computer's off, maybe they could turn it on—I don't know, I'm assuming they can. And I think when we don't know, we assume they can because we've seen it done in movies, and we've heard it talked about. We hear that our planes can be hacked into, that there are these conferences where people hack pacemakers and, frankly, it all just seems like magic, and everything seems possible.

My high school installed a program called DyKnow, and I hated it. It allowed them to monitor our computers in some way, but none of us were exactly sure what it could and could not do. I had one teacher who would routinely pull up the computer screens of people who stayed home sick from school to show the class what they were doing. "Ah, look, she's writing an email to her aunt!" he'd comment cheerfully, reading a few lines. I resented the Orwellian omnipotence DyKnow had over us. We weren't sure what it could and could not do, so we didn't know how to avoid it. The teachers claimed that it shut down after school ended, but how could we be sure this was true? Girls were constantly getting in trouble for what they did online after hours—who could say it wasn't DyKnow that caught them? We lived in constant fear of DyKnow, worried that teachers would read our complaints about them on our screens or catch us playing games online during class. We didn't know the limitations of DyKnow, and so it seemed to us that it could do anything and everything. It was powerful precisely because it was so shadowy. I've graduated and have a new computer now, DyKnow-free (hopefully), but I've never lost that fear of being watched. I have no idea what is possible online, so I assume everything is. The myths shed some light on the situation, but I have no way of knowing if they are accurate or not.

As we become more and more linked to our lives online, it becomes increasingly important to examine the myths we live by. What really works and what doesn't? It scares me that I don't know. Since I don't know, I assume that someone must have handled it, that it must not be a threat or more people would know about it. This creates a cycle of personal ignorance in which I do not even know what I don't know. It creates a culture of disbelief. I'm online everyday, constantly linked in; therefore, I surely would be aware if there was something hugely threatening about it.

Yet there is a fear there, behind everyone's calm. My ten-year-old cousin loves these little online multi-player games like Club Penguin and Moshi Monsters. She and her brother and sister play them all the time; and, when they heard I was working on this book, they were happy to show me around their accounts. She talked happily and easily about the mini-games and decorating her house, clearly within her comfort zone, and I remembered being her age and playing these games, too. My aunt, trying to steer the conversation more towards cybercrime for me, told her to talk about the time she woke up in the middle of the night.

My cousin froze up. She didn't want to talk about it, and told my aunt that she didn't want to remember it since it made her feel guilty. She felt this guilt because she was still so worried that she was going to be the cause of one of those terrible stories on the news. My articulate, smiley, happy cousin was scared, and I had never seen her so speechless before. My aunt explained for her: she had made a list of her friends and their usernames, connecting their real name to their online handle on Moshi Monsters. She woke up that night panicked that this would lead to her friends' demise, and felt so guilty to have broken one of the mythical rules of the Internet that she still didn't want to speak of it all these months later. She made me promise not to use her name.

At first, I thought it was sweet that she was scared. How adorably innocent, I thought. I remembered being ten, and being scared. And then, as I inboxed a friend on Facebook about why I deleted a post of hers off my timeline, I realized that I was every bit as paranoid as my little cousin. But why wasn't I more afraid? I was clearly aware that there are threats out there, that there are indeed people watching—why else would I censor my own Facebook page? However, despite all the reasons I should be scared, all the statistics that should terrify me, I found that I wasn't afraid. Why? Well, in part, I think it's because I'm just so used to it. It's so pedestrian that it seems it couldn't possibly be dangerous. We're so used to living in this constantly monitored world where we assume we are always watched, that I think we forget to think about who's watching.

A girl in my neighborhood was in the paper for some reason. She won a tournament, and so they put her in the paper. A man saw her photo and her name in the paper, and he found her on Facebook and figured out not only where she had been but where she was going to be in a week. She was headed to another golf tournament, and he met her there. He told her that he saw her in the paper and that he had found her, and she freaked out. Of course she freaked out.

It's scary. He meant well. He wasn't a genius or anything (clearly, or he wouldn't have told her that he found her in the paper); he wasn't some techie, he was just a creepy guy with a newspaper subscription and Internet. Anyone can do this—anyone! It seems like hackers are these magicians who live in basements, secluded like hermits from the rest of the world, whom you've never met in everyday life because they live on a diet of Cheetos and comics and they're some antiquated stereotype from the Simpsons—and then suddenly you realize that it's you! I learned somewhere that many Facebook users display their username in the address of their page, and a quick Google search on this username usually shows you much about them. It's public information and you can find it, and so you realize that hackers aren't something magical but instead something that's part of the everyday.

And there are so many people to be afraid of, why am I not more afraid? I know that stuff like this is possible; I've heard other stories like this, so why am I not more scared? People tell me these things, and I still feel safe. Well, first, I feel safe because I'm insignificant, a speck in a sea of millions of people. Why stalk me? There's no good reason to stalk me. I'm just some girl, and you could find some girl anywhere, online or off. But wait, my insignificance is my biggest security measure? How dangerous is that? My entire defense strategy cannot be to stay below the radar of bad guys.

As I picked apart my feeling of security further, I realized that there was much more to it. The truth is, there's an entire wall between me and the danger, because of a set of rules I follow. I don't go on those websites—the dark corners of the Internet they say are renowned for malware. I have a Mac, which they say can't get viruses—and, as I listen to myself, I realize that the wall is imagined, composed solely of social convention, its bricks and mortar purely mythical. And I realize that I am afraid—terrified, in fact. I'm not afraid of someone hacking my computer to steal my identity, but I am afraid of the massive power of the Internet, a power I cannot quite understand. Because I can't understand it, I retreat back into my world of myths, where I feel safe. And so the cycle repeats, with my exiting Plato's cave only long enough to be blinded before diving back into the shadows.

We will never be made to believe the sky is falling. Our digital world's sky is supported by a mythology, a mythology that assures us that it cannot all crumble before us. Be it Google, Anonymous, or the government, someone will save us. There is no way the cyber infrastructure could collapse, no way for the online banks to fail, for all the money to be lost, for the stocks to crash completely, for everything to go completely and entirely and irreversibly wrong.

We will never believe in an apocalypse.

And so, when people tell us that these things can happen, a natural first response is just: no. No, that can't happen. But it can happen. It is possible, it's been demonstrated, it can be done.

We are not, however, entirely wrong in our sense of security. It can happen, in the same way that the plane we are boarding can crash. Like the plane, it probably won't, at least not today. And, just like the plane, there are reasons for this. There are safety measures in place. But these measures can fail. There are things that seem too terrible to be true. Unfortunately, this does not make them impossible.

Gene Spafford Interview
Director: CERIAS
Purdue University
Summer 2012

~ CN ~

What do I see as possible futures? To answer this, you first have to put it into context; take a larger view of security and why we have a problem.

In the 1950s and '60s computers were very, very expensive. The first in equivalent dollars today cost $24 million. They required huge investments, and so they were shared. Lots of research went into how to protect these systems. From the 1950s to the 1980s the fear was the "Red Menace"—The Insider Threat. In the late 1970s people came to the conclusion that this was an "undecidable problem"—that it was impossible to find (and thus secure) all the problems. So much of the money dried up. In the 1980s not a lot of money was put into practical testing and security.

But computers continued to develop. Rapidly. And they got cheaper and cheaper. In the 1990s, then, the computing community had to grow expertise to create and build the software and systems needed for this explosion in technology. Money reared its head again. Given this situation, the market decided to buy what was needed to add to existing systems. But additions aren't sufficient—we are still using the "sharing" paradigm developed decades before. This was true across the board: Windows, Linux, everyone—the sharing paradigm is still in place. This holds true at the most basic level: Windows and Linux are used in building systems, and they are building in this original sharing framework at the foundations of systems used today. So the ideology is kind of locked in. But we know we can't fully secure such a system.

My take on all this is that we need to change the paradigm and build a new form of system. But people say we can't do it, and it is questionable that they'd give up their legacy systems even if we succeeded in making something better.

So we add on to the existing software, and this makes things slower; new hardware is developed, and this makes the system faster, and then we have capacity to add on new software—the cycle goes on. Security is never adequately addressed or solved in this cycle.

Building "hardened systems"—multi-level ones secure for the military—developed in the earlier days of computers, and then in the 1980s computers exploded into civilian business, something that had not been fully expected. Who back in the early days thought that the entire base of virtually all business, communication, and entertainment would be digital?

Viruses really took off in the late 1980s and 1990s. At first security professionals tried to harden systems with anti-virus software, but that didn't really work against all the threats. So attention turned to firewalls; then to "intrusion-detection" systems; then "encryption"; then "extrusion-detection"; and then "extrusion-prevention." Now we are beginning to see companies offering two sets of services: One, pen-testers who try to find vulnerabilities in company networks that can be exploited so as to fix them; and two, after a company has been hacked and lost valuable resources, the security firm will help identify what was lost and rebuild the company's systems.

This ecosystem doesn't really make sense, and it is driven by short-term economics—as well as the fact that people don't understand risk and reality. People are either in denial, or unknowing—they are not dumb.

There is a lack of internalization of risk. Even if people are apprised of the risks, they seem to be responding with the attitude that "it can't happen to me! We put a firewall in place." There are economic ramifications to what they do, and they don't understand them.

I was an EMT, and worked in a hospital emergency room—I know what havoc the unexpected can cause, how people hold ideas about risk that "it can't happen to them," and what it's like when it does happen to them. It's also similar to gambling—when belief out-competes reality.

I think that, at present, not enough people have had bad experiences to get to a level of general awareness and outrage where change will begin in earnest.

So, back to the future and possible scenarios. In about 1996 I gave a talk at the FBI where I said that we'll see escalations in vigilante-ism and private actions in dealing with cybercrime and security-breeches. When I made those predictions, the FBI said I was crazy. I still stand by these predictions; in some ways you could say they are a new emerging norm, with a half-dozen major companies in this space, one of which was co-founded by an ex-FBI assistant director!

Looking at the bigger picture, there are a number of ways things can go.

To begin with, chances are that what's coming could be much worse than what we are anticipating. Black Swan events—meaning the unlikely, the unexpected—can occur and could cause all kinds of catastrophic events. Consider a non-computing example—the Katka volcano in Iceland. There has not been a major eruption in modern times, but it is still active, and we have geologic evidence of what it can do. If it goes off in a major way, the particles in the air will be carried on air currents widely over Europe, and force a stop of air traffic. If this goes on long enough (a long eruption), governments relying on inter/national air transport and trade, and on air force support and security, can falter, even fall. Economies would be profoundly affected, and would suffer and decline. There might be famine, disease. In such conditions, would major conflicts occur with NATO unable to respond, like a war between Israel and Iran? Who has thought through scenarios such as this? People cannot predict the possible extent of effects of totally unexpected events, and we certainly don't prepare for them.

Here's a possible not-so-great future resulting from poor cyber-security: we could see the growth of criminal syndicates or anarchists that either intentionally or unintentionally set the conditions that topple governments, and bring about great instability. That could lead to all sorts of possible scenarios; for example, China could fragment into smaller countries, North Korea could attack South Korea, Pakistan could launch nuclear weapons against India....These are all things that might be facilitated by prolonged cyber operations. In the USA the agenda of the "sovereign citizen" and white supremists could be fueled by controlling and extending dialogues of division and hate online. You cannot say there is a non-zero chance of a future where these groups erupt. Or, consider another possibility: there are tens of thousands of people under government contract building cyber-offensive capabilities—if the economy tanks for some reason, what do you predict they'd do? Will they all be honest when they can't feed their families? There are many possible scenarios with bad outcomes if the wrong players are involved and circumstances fall their way.

On the other hand, better outcomes are possible. Personally, I don't think it's all going to tank—it's recoverable. We learned a (partial) lesson with viruses and worms.

This is a framing issue. You can only solve problems you've properly defined. If security is framed as a military problem, then the society has to turn everything over to the military for solutions. The political mindset in the USA now tends to be: these problems are "more than cyber." There's the belief that these problems are big, certainly, but that the only way to handle them is to let the military take care of them; that this is an existential problem.

This may or may not be an existential issue—but if cyber-security is defined purely as a military issue, we may be investing in a set of solutions that may not be taking us any closer to where we need to be.

People in power see "expertise equals financial investment equals success," and this isn't right, especially when knowledge is really power. These are not problems we can solve solely by technology.

We have to address social issues because all these issues of security are embedded in social realities and societal systems. These can't be cured by technology—but by people. Technology plays a role, but we have to educate people, develop new social systems, sensibilities, and the like.

There are three ways to influence people's behaviors:

1) change the environment—fund work on safer systems and greater deployment;

2) increase/decrease penalties/rewards in official capacities;
3) create social pressures and norms: the force of society, of etiquette, mores, religion.

It's a problem if the third way is not the dominant force of change because it is needed for the other two. We absorb technology, we use it, we flow around it, envelop it—it can't change us. It's the social structures and the dynamism of society that define how we develop. How much pain will we go through? It all depends on the political and economic types of solutions forged within societies—like defining cyber-security as a military problem when it isn't.

I have a certain amount of hope. Why does society function as well as it does? Most people are largely good and moral. For instance, in the USA there are lots of gun owners, but there is not chaos and blood running in the streets daily because the majority of people are sane. The majority of people are trying to find the moral path to do what they want to do.

The fact that Black Hat exists shows that people are trying to forge a moral path. The fact that hackers get together and talk about moral frameworks—and that they warn of dangerous hacks—is itself a moral act. I believe most people are like this, if only we encourage it.

Given enough sharing of education and information, we will reach a point where we can accommodate and deal with cyber-problems, although we can never eliminate them all. You were talking about beginning to learn about hacking first to stay safe when you were targeted, and then for this book, and how many average kids working in the computer department of Walmart or strangers such as a person behind a hotel check-in would take some time to teach you something. The simple fact that you can go into

Black Hat and Walmart and people knowledgeable about hacking and security will share with you what you need shows the caring inherent in the system.

THE PROBLEM WITH DEFINITIONS
~ CN ~

> 1ST SPEAKER: "A SECURITY MATRIX IS A TOTAL WHANKER
> WASTE OF TIME. LIKE JACK DANIELS SAID, STATISTICS
> ARE ABOUT AS VALUABLE AS ME SAYING MY CAT WEIGHS
> 130 MILES PER HOUR."
>
> 2ND SPEAKER: "AND THAT'S WHAT WE CALL THE
> SCIENTIFIC METHOD."
>
> — DISCUSSION AT BLACKHAT 2011 KEYNOTE

IF THE NET "SMASHES" geographic borders, as the security giant McAfee writes, it also shatters conceptual boundaries.

Time-honored definitions of war, crime, threat, solution, and power simply don't work in the cyber-universe.

All too often, Stefano Zanero cautions, we turn to metaphors for understanding the cyber-universe(s) unfolding among us.[1] At the most basic level, he explains, the term cybernetics was wedded to the concept of space to produce cyberspace:

> But this is a metaphor, not a reality. Factually, there is no cyber "space."
>
> For example, *website* is a metaphor. It is an illusion. The physics

of what is taking place are different from what terms like these convey. These provide a way for humans to comprehend things, but metaphors do not exist physically.

There are real repercussions, Zanero continues: for example, how do you define cyberspace as the 4th domain of war? The traditional three—sea, land, and air—are real, tangible, physical. But cyberspace is a metaphor. How can we wage war in cyberspace? Zanero counts off his fingers as he explains:

First, it's not metric.

Second, it's not a space—and I mean that in the sense that humans understand space as something you can move into. It is a matrix of connected servers and routers and "things" and "stuff" that exists not by "itself," but because these are privately owned by businesses.

And third, unlike the first three domains of war, cyberspace can't exist regardless of humans.

If we think cyberspace is space we are thinking badly, because we are thinking of something that doesn't exist. Thinking of this matrix of servers and routers and "things" owned by private companies over the globe as the "4th domain of war" is an illusion—a dangerous one.

This one thing—mistaking cyberspace metaphors for actual space of war—might start WW3.[2]

"On the Internet, you can radically re-purpose yourself. You can create change; and you can do this so that there is no forensic past.

"Think of a person's physical presence: it must exist within the limits of physics. But digitally, a person can multi-purpose, and they can do so rapidly and radically, and then they can re-multi-purpose."

— Aaron Striegel[3]

This is just the beginning of the complications. We lack definitions at the most basic level for realities like war, crime, economic value, and law in the emerging era. If someone hacks a person's pacemaker to kill them, it might be murder, or it might be assassination—depending on who was killed.[4] If deemed to be the latter, new laws implemented in the USA in 2011 now uphold the country's right to retaliate militarily to a cyber-attack. These are not idle questions:

> The fatal car crash of journalist Michael Hastings in June 2013 is "consistent with a car cyber-attack," Richard Clarke, former U.S. National Coordinator for Security, Infrastructure Protection and Counter-terrorism, stated.[5]

Cases have occurred in a number of countries worldwide where criminals have held important computer systems or data for ransom; or have disrupted public infrastructure as a smokescreen for a cyber-bank robbery. To retaliate militarily on the sovereign nation where the criminals reside invites political nightmares.

That is, if the origin of the attack can be confirmed. The Net carrying any code from one computer to another is a vast inter-penetrating flux of global movement and exchange. Dropping a piece of malware into the maelstrom amid the trillions of pieces of data dropping in simultaneously worldwide can make pinpoint attribution most difficult.

Problems don't stop here. In 2010 and 2011 massive international cyber-intrusions came to light such as "Night Dragon" into major energy companies, and "Shady Rat's" penetration of governments, non-governmental organizations, and industries worldwide. "Critical infrastructure" from Lockheed Martin and nuclear reactors through NASDAC and related financial institutions to the Pentagon and military have been broached. The examples multiply exponentially. By 2012 General Keith Alexander, USCYBERCOM commander and NSA Director, said in a DefCon keynote:

> They're in. That's the starting point. Get used to it. The question now is: How do we deal with this?

Are these criminal acts of selling knowledge to the highest bidder? Espionage? And, if so, by whom: nation-states, transnational criminal enterprises brokering data, non-state actors, terrorists, competing industries? Or do they constitute military threats? Or all of the above in some new 21st-century set of power-configurations, where transnational criminal enterprises conduct cyber-intrusions for data they can variously broker with governments, sell to corporate buyers, and make available to non-state actors for economic gain and political control?

And what happens when we factor in the sophisticated cyber-markets where individuals worldwide can buy intrusive software, the hacker-expertise to employ it, and the darknet connections to sell it for myriad purposes? This adds not hundreds, not thousands, but millions of "wild cards" whose actions may ultimately trigger activities deemed threatening to nation-states regardless of the person's intent.

Worse, unlike an F-35 fighter plane, a ball-bearing, or a dollar bill, *data*—the diagrammatics of the F-35 and account flows controlling dollars—can be sold and resold, shared and simultaneously used by many anywhere in the world. This changes the fundamental definition of value at the core of our economic systems.

Where are the neat definitions of war, criminality, economic value, and sovereign power in all this? Where do we turn for realistic new definitions—ones that are not hype, hysteria, myth, and politics?

Endnotes

[1] Interview at Black Hat 2012 conference, 7/26/2012.

[2] See also: Adriane Lapointe, "When Good Metaphors Go Bad, The Metaphoric 'Branding' of Cyberspace," Washington DC: Center for Strategic & International Studies, *http://www.csis.org/tech*. Accessed 5/25/2012.

[3] Aaron Striegel, Electrical Engineering/Computer Security, University of Notre Dame. Personal Communication 12/15/12.

[4] Barnaby Jack, a well-known and widely respected white-hack hacker, was famed for, among other things, showing how malicious attacks can be made on implanted medical technology. He died suddenly just before giving his latest presentation at Black Hat 2013, explaining to Reuters the week before:

> [H]e had devised a way to hack into a wireless communications system that linked implanted pacemakers and defibrillators with bedside monitors that gather information about their operations.

http://news.yahoo/famed-hacker-barnaby-jack-dies-week-before-hacking-convention. Accessed 7/29/2013.

[5] Kurt Nimmo, "Richard Clarke: Hastings Accident 'Consistent with a Car Cyber Attack,'" *Infowars*, June 24, 2013, *http://www.infowars.com/richard-clarke-hastings-accident-consistent-with-a-car-cyber-attack/*. Accessed 7/19/2013. Citing research by the Center for Automotive Embedded Systems Security published in 2011, the news release further explained:

> Currently, there's nothing to stop anyone with malicious intent and some computer-programming skills from taking command of your vehicle. After gaining access, a hacker could control everything from which song plays on the radio to whether the brakes work.

The Self

~ LC ~

SOMEWHERE AMONG THE MASSIVE influx of information on the Internet, there is the individual. Billions of individuals, actually, all adrift in this cyber-world—little snippets of their selfhood encased in online information. What does it mean to be a denizen of the digital age? For the individual, the Internet is a powerful force in the everyday. It allows for better communication and better access to information, and is perhaps the invention that has had the single most profound impact on life this century. However, with all this good comes some evil. The Internet changes life for the individual, and not always for the better. The environment is changing rapidly, and with it, I believe the self is readjusting its expression and understanding of its own selfhood. The Internet is not some separate realm, distinct from the everyday, but rather another layer over the physical world. It permeates the "real world" even as that world shapes and creates it. People have to exist within this complex and dynamic relationship, and the failure to navigate it successfully can be nothing short of social suicide.

Cyber-bullying is a good illustration of the way the Internet affects the individual. It is not the addition of some new, foreign concept so much as it is the expansion of an old problem. There is a lot of buzz around cyber-bullying, and I think, personally, that it is something that is very misunderstood. From the limited local news specials I've seen on it, it appears that many people, adults especially, are viewing cyber-bullying as more of a Second-Life scenario. In this point of view, people tend to picture children's avatars being bullied by other avatars online. They imagine that strangers, who have met and become friends with the children online, begin to attack the kids verbally online, embarrassing and shaming the children. The other tendency is to view cyber-bullying as some new evil enabled by this strange new technology. Otherwise nice children are tempted to become monsters online, proponents of this view seem to say, because of the anonymity or the distance from the person or what have you.

The mistake people are making here is imagining that somehow a child's online life is a separate entity from their everyday life. Rather than isolated incidents of a kid from school posting something online, or a stranger saying something on Xbox Live, I think that the worst cyber-bullying is typically the extension of real-time, real-life bullying. It is not a new thing, born of this devilish new technology, but rather an old evil. Kids can be mean, and the Internet just gives them another outlet for a cruelty that has existed long before the cyber.

Before, a friend would get in a fight with a friend, and she would call that friend a name, or share an embarrassing secret, or so forth. Something regrettable would be said, it would be hurtful, and there would be a fight over it; but when it went away, there wouldn't be a public record. Because it was said and not written, it fades eventually, preserved only by memory. On the Internet, nothing fades.

Not only can a temporary outburst online be archived, private conversations can quickly become very public. An increasing problem with the Internet is that you are linked into everything. So let's say that, instead of saying something nasty about a friend to someone, you put it on your mutual friend's wall. Well, all of a sudden, all of your friends have seen it. It gets circled back to the person. It's public, and it's indisputable because it's there, in black and white text blinking on a screen.

You wouldn't typically have a fight in a crowded room. You wouldn't stand in the middle of the gym floor at a pep rally and just hurl insults at someone.

But that's what Facebook and Twitter end up being—everyone's there, and everyone's watching. In fact, both sites teach you to desire and demand an audience. They count likes or retweets, allowing everyone to see the popularity of your every post, and friend and follower counts encourage people to be less private to seem more popular. So let's say that you tweet a joke at your friend's expense to get a few laughs, or maybe a few favorites on your tweet. Before Twitter, that would just be a joke shared between friends; but now, anyone and everyone who could possibly be interested can see it. I think that's one of the dangers of the Internet—you're speaking immediately to what could conceivably end up being the entire world. Now, most of the time it isn't. Most people only are so interested in the fact that you think so and so is a fat slob—the world at large is very minimally interested. However, the people that you care about, and the people whose opinion of you directly affects you probably are going to care. Your friends, your crush, your classmates, and even possibly your family all could see this, and all of a sudden you're in the guidance counselor's office.

I went to an all-girls high school, and so you can probably imagine that this occasionally got out of hand. We used to have a huge problem with a website called Formspring in my high school. Formspring is a site that allows people to ask questions and have people respond anonymously, and the grade below me was obsessed with it. Girls at my school liked to post questions like "How do you really feel about me?" on it. Why they would do this, I have no idea. The guidance counselors apparently had set up an account to see if the rumors were true, and were so shocked by what they saw that they called all the people involved down to the counselor's office. Anyway, we had to have an assembly called because girls were posting this question and getting answers back to the effect of "I hate you; go kill yourself."

Would you say that in real life? I'm tempted to say no. I guess I'm not privy to a lot of these conversations, so maybe they are said in private and I just don't know about it, whereas I can see it if it's posted online or read aloud during an assembly, but I'd like to think this isn't the case. I also think the context matters. There is no way you would say that in a crowded room with a lot of people watching. You wouldn't say it in front of a teacher or a parent. You probably wouldn't even say it in front of a classmate you didn't know very well. Maybe, conceivably, you would say it in front of a small group of people you knew pretty well, but you would not say it in front of the entire school. What I noticed was that this ended up being in front of the entire school. This wasn't the typical feud where two parties fought and a small group of people knew about it while the world at large remained ignorant.

What does this social panopticon mean for the self? How can identity be constructed when there are algorithms designed to tell you exactly who you are and what you are going to do? What does the future hold for issues of privacy and personhood? In many ways, I think the Internet is good for the individual. It opens doors, and allows the individual access to previously unobtainable things. The everyman, for instance, probably would not have been able to easily gain a good understanding of the Higgs Boson independently of the newspapers. With the Internet, I was able to find articles written by physicists about it, and Google every word and method mentioned that I didn't understand, breaking it into progressively smaller and smaller pieces until I finally was able to piece together what all this talk of a God particle was about. I'm no physics major, so even my college courses would never have prepared me to be able to talk about it.

This access to information is not inconsequential. You can, while sitting at your computer, never moving an inch, learn about almost anything you can think of. Many elite universities have begun to put their class lectures online for free. Experts opine on almost everything online, making it easy to get a sense of not only what the information is but also how people have been interpreting it and using it. TED talks—a series of inspirational videos about Technology, Entertainment, and Design—allow you to listen to some of the greatest minds in the world talk about their areas of passion. It doesn't have to be in your major, you don't have to worry about fitting it into your schedule, it's just you, in your free time, learning for free. Free information. If you have the motivation, you can learn. Now, you won't get the certification from the university saying that you've learned unless you're enrolling in official online courses, but you still have the information. I don't think there has ever before been the opportunity to be so well-versed in so many things so easily and so quickly.

The Internet also puts a lot of power in the hands of the people. Google bombing, for instance, can be a very democratic process. Large groups of people who share a viewpoint try to influence the

Google algorithm by linking terms together repeatedly, such as the battle for the top result of "miserable failure" being either George Bush or Michael Moore. "The man" is being broken down. Musicians don't need to get a record label. If their YouTube channel makes them famous, then they're famous, and they don't need to convince a record executive that they have potential. The same is beginning to be true for authors, who can self-publish online and build a name for themselves without having to break into the traditional publishing industry.

It's a double-edged sword, this new technology of ours. It can allow us to reach untold heights, but that also makes it much more dangerous to fall. The immediate access to a large audience can be a boon or a bane. Our close contact with friends can be great for staying in contact but awful for any hope we had of privacy. Even outside of considering cybercrime, there are many dangers online. The possibilities are almost infinite, and not all of the outcomes are good. Information becomes a weapon, whether it is personal information about someone or just Internet know-how, but there is nothing stopping the individual from being well-armed.

For the first time since the social contract grouped people into societies, the individual stands on the same level as the collective. Armies could be halted if one knew the correct code. The future is limitless, for better or worse. With great power comes great responsibility, and, as the cyber brings the knowledgeable one step closer to superhuman, we have a lot of redefining to do.

PART TWO

THE HACK-NET

The Hack
~ CN ~

Speaker 1:
"I was so proud of my 10-year-old niece this week. We were all sitting around talking—she's on her iPhone and she puts it down saying, 'I just hacked the iPhone.' Yup, she's 10."

Speaker 2:
"My 10-year-old daughter knows JavaScript and she can use it to get into all the core systems of hotels."

— Plenary discussion, Black Hat 2011

Anything that involves computer code can be hacked. Laptops, smartphones, cars, pacemakers, Air Force drones, security alarm systems, factory assembly lines, robots. Jerome Radcliffe hacked his own kidney dialysis machine at the podium in the Black Hat 2011 conference to show how easy, and dangerous, this is.

Hackers hate the word "hack" and use it anyway. Non-hackers use the word without really knowing what it means. The security industry uses it in reports because there is simply no other word that captures the imagination and reality of something that is so profoundly changing the world.

The word has deep caché.[1]

The evolution of the hack is dramatic. Originally hackers built, tested, broke, and rebuilt the world of computing as we know it. They hacked the analog and created the digital. The best were seen as creative, or rogue, geniuses. They knew code, could analyze it for vulnerabilities, write new code to exploit these, and gain access into closed systems—a back window left open in a locked house so to speak. Profit had little to do with this.

Hacking forums were a new town square where people gathered to share camaraderie and the news of the day—code, exploits, solutions, new frontiers. Here, the teenager who got into the Department of Defense's website and the top security researcher for a large company could sit side by side sharing a metaphorical beer in virtual conversation.

Then for-profit was born.

While security companies like McAfee and Kaspersky refined anti-virus software with the information tossed up by hackers, others bundled the code into a booming global business selling spyware, malware, surveillance-ware, crime-ware and the like.[2]

"The hack" was irrevocably changed at this point. People with absolutely no coding skills nor computer expertise could get an app and install it.

At the low end, scores of websites sell spyware for individual computers and phones for as little as $19.00, sometimes on sale for $9.99. For this pittance, you can listen to your target's calls, have copies of their text messages sent to your phone, download their contact lists, call records, surfing history, IMs, pictures, videos, and the like onto your system, and GPS them for location, among other things. For a few dollars more you can move up to a more deluxe package that also includes the ability to turn their machine or phone on and off, activate a listening program when they are not on the phone, turn on the webcam, take and send pictures back to you.

At the high end—and often this is under a thousand dollars—DIY (Do It Yourself) kits are available to build your own botnet to infect and control an army of unsuspecting zombie computers owned by average users around the globe. If you don't have the expertise to use the software yourself, "hackers-for-hire" are a booming business. The infected "bots," or zombie computers are controlled remotely by your computer, and with older tried and true popular programs like Zeus, SpyEye, and NeoSploit, and new ones continuously added, you have full access to everything on the target's computer, including the ability to run clandestine activities from the infected bot. In most cases, the user is never aware they have been hit.

A botmaster can control anywhere from hundreds to millions of zombies. The higher-end versions are sophisticated, and relatively cheap, considering fifty years ago entire intelligence agencies required legions of spies physically planting bugs in order to get far less information than a single malware program can collect today.

More specialized intrusion-ware can be designed to infiltrate specific military, security, government, and business sites. Custom versions of these malware programs can be built to target specific people and industries. As one hacker anonymously explains:

> I can buy data on a CEO or a government official if I don't want to research them myself.
>
> All I need to find out is a few basics, easily available on the net or from a simple bit of social engineering: who he gets email from that he trusts—his family, friends, business associates, club members, whatever.
>
> Then I send the CEO or the official or military commander an

email with malware to his iPhone, ostensibly from a person or place they trust without giving it a second thought. Then I drop on a rootkit to take full remote control of the device.

I can now access his calendar, appointments, notes, texts, calls— but today, let's say, I'm most interested in his calendar: I want to know when his private, highly classified meeting is.

With full control of his phone, I simply turn it on when he enters the "high level, high security" meeting, and switch on audio, and perhaps the video. *Voilà*, I have his latest and most sensitive business or government or military—or even personal—information.

I can use it, sell it, blackmail him. Perhaps, instead, I decide to change, or delete, some of his confidential business data, [or] run a misinformation campaign.

He leaves the meeting; I go with him, wherever he goes.

New intrusive malware is released with remarkable speed and frequency that revolutionizes stealing money and data from financial institutions; harvesting data in industrial and governmental espionage; creating "social-bots" to troll Online Social Networks collecting users' personal information; and, in the post-*Stuxnet* era, controlling or causing physical damage to critical infrastructure.

New breakthroughs of "what is possible, even thinkable" are taking place at digital, not analog, speed. Many accept that the barrier of what is considered "hack-able" has been completely erased—anything Net-connect-able.[3]

Of course, attacks don't go unchallenged. After fighting unsuccessfully for years to keep intruders out of their systems, people are now considering new options. Founder Jeff Moss opened the Black Hat 2012 conference with the challenge:

How far can, and should, people, companies and governments go in returning fire against an attack? Should targets of cyber-attacks retaliate against intruders instead of just trying to protect their own assets? If so, what are the acceptable parameters of intrusive attack, and what crosses the line into co-equivalent criminality or risks dangerous levels of escalation, possibly to national levels?

While many of these conversations are going on behind closed doors, the country of Georgia brought it onto the international stage in 2012. The country suffered a targeted attack against the government's ministerial computers, especially those with military concerns. The Georgian Computer Emergency Response Team traced the malware back to hackers in Russia. They then created a virus of their own to infect the Russian hacker's computer that, among other things, was able to take pictures of him. As the computer security engineer Dirk Van Bruggen noted to me in an email about this: "Whether the information is accurate or not, the big thing is that the Georgians posted information about their hack on the hacker before they could catch him."

At the same time this was taking place in late 2012, U.S. banks were coming under a series of cyber-attacks more interested in disrupting the financial centers' operations than in theft. A number of analysts pointed out that the attacks may have originated in Iranian retaliation for the USA's 2010 Stuxnet cyber-attack that incapacitated Iranian nuclear reactors.

This is set in the context of another seismic shift in the "hack's evolution": in 2011, cyber-attacks formally escalated into the theatre of war. The USA declared that cyber-attacks against critical infrastructure—which includes banking and financial systems as well as energy, transport, communication, and defense—constitute an act of war that can justify both cyber and conventional military (kinetic) retaliation.

=✳=

"Que. [Quebec, Montreal] boy, 12, pleads guilty to hacking government websites."

— Michael Nguyen, *Toronto Sun*[4]

At present, the world has more kinds and numbers of hacks taking place than definitions to make sense of them.

We are enacting what we don't know how to talk about yet. White-hat security (the proverbial good, legal), black-hat exploits (the proverbial bad, illegal), crime, war, innovation, vigilante justice—the words bleed and blend into one another—language that little matches the realities it is supposed to speak to.

Even the foundational word *hack* is simultaneously eschewed, banned, ridiculed, over-determined, under-defined, embraced, and ubiquitous.

Hacking is perhaps unique among human endeavors—the only behavior used equally by inventors, heroes, and rogues; by the dangerously criminal, the pedantically helpful, the mundane, and the visionary. It is defined by all of these, and thus by none.

Born in action and not in theory, *hack* may usher in the post-definitional.

Endnotes

[1] It is not possible to cite the full range of anthropological work on hacking; for a good place to start, see Gabriella Coleman's work on hackers, Tom Boellstroff's on virtual life, and Alessandro Delfanti's on bio-hacking.

[2] Individuals can buy these wares easily and cheaply on the Internet, and can load them covertly onto anyone's computer and cellphone and gain full access. Businesses can buy these to monitor their employees. Clandestine groups can buy them for surveillance. Companies can buy them for industrial espionage. Governments can use these to monitor citizens. Try a simple Web search on words such as "cell phone spy," "computer surveillance," or "cheating spouse? Monitor your kids for drugs" for inexpensive commercial products. See Krebs on Security for excellent coverage of global-level crime-ware commerce.

[3] As I write this in the Fall of 2013, Dragos Ruiu and the malware "badBIOS" he is battling are capturing cyber-attention. The story is emblematic of this era of unprecedented techno-discoveries. Ruiu speculates the malware infects the BIOS (Basic Input/Output System) and UEFI (Unified Extensible Firmware Interface)—the lowest levels of computer hardware—transmitted through a USB drive. It appears to jump "air-gapped" (physically as well as digitally separated) machines, to have "self-healing" capabilities—and, possibly, to use ultra-high-frequency transmissions from computers' speakers and microphones to communicate with other air-gapped computers. Dan Goodin writes that this seems the stuff of a post-apocalyptic movie, but is being seriously considered given Ruiu's reputation. Until more data emerges, security experts seem equally prepared to accept badBIOS as an unwitting hoax or a new level of malware that pushes back the boundaries of what is deemed "possible."

Dan Goodin, "Meet 'badBIOS,' the mysterious Mac and PC malware that jumps airgaps," *Ars Technica*, October 31, 2013, *http://arstechnica.com/security/2013/10/meet-badbios-the-mysterious-mac-and-pc-malware-that-jumps-airgaps.* Accessed 11/1/2013.

See also Dragos Ruiu's Twitter, Facebook, and Google Plus sites documenting his investigation of "badBIOS."

[4] Michael Nguyen, "Que. boy, 12, pleads guilty to hacking government websites," *Toronto Sun*, October 25, 2013, *http://www.torontosun.com/2013/10/25/que-boy-pleads-guilty*. Accessed 10/25/2013.

Charlie Miller Interview
Inside the Hack
~ LC ~

THE MORE I LEARNED about hacking, the more I discovered I knew nothing about it. In an attempt to understand how hacking actually works, I turned to Dr. Charlie Miller, a Notre Dame alumnus with a PhD in mathematics who worked as a security analyst and global network exploitation analyst for the National Security Agency for years.

Miller is both a security analyst and a hacker famous for his hacks on Apple products—the cyber equivalent of someone who breaks banks to reveal potential security breaches. "Companies hire me to look at their code and look at what they're working on, look at their products and try to find qualms with them so they can fix them and release products that are at least a little harder to break into," Miller says. "They're not going to be perfect, but a little tougher." He was the first to find a bug in the MacBook Air in the Pwn2Own competition and, perhaps even more famously, was also the first to release a remote hack for the iPhone. He hacked the MacBook Air in two minutes, but is careful to clarify that hacking is not something that occurs spontaneously and quickly. Rather, it is the result of months of careful research. As he says, "You can't do it without a ton of preparation."

The potential results of that preparation are incredible. Take, for instance, what Miller's remote hack on the iPhone allowed him to do: "On the original iPhone exploit I wrote, if I could get the user to end up on my webpage somehow, then I could take control of their browser and, back then, the browser ran with full privileges, so I could do whatever. I could steal photos or contacts, or make the phone dial somebody, or send a text message, or turn the microphone on—anything, really. I could do anything the user could do, and then probably more stuff."

Web exploits can similarly take over a complete computer, and can continue to run even after the web browser is closed. If the browser uses sandboxing, like Google Chrome does, it adds another hurdle for the attacker to overcome, but is still not impenetrable. Miller explains it mathematically: instead of having to find just one bug to run an exploit, the hacker now has to find two, which means that, if there is a ten percent chance of finding a bug in a certain amount of time, the chance of finding two bugs in that time are now closer to one percent. While there are ways of making it exponentially more difficult for someone to write an exploit, there is no foolproof way to secure a web browser completely from these attacks. The implications are astounding—someone can remotely control your computer without your ever being aware of it, track your keystrokes, and turn on your web camera.

Miller is well aware of these threats, but he doesn't let them faze him. "I know enough to know that it [my computer] could certainly get broken into everyday, and there is nothing I can really do about it," he says. He compares it to knowing a missile could hit your house at any moment—you know it *could* happen, but there is no real reason it *would* and, besides, there is little you can do about it anyway. "I try to not present much of a target," he says. "I try to be nice to everyone." By taking a few precautions, he protects himself against some of the threats, but says that anyone who really wanted to could probably find a way into his computer.

"Sophistication has to meet motivation," Miller says. The people who know how to do these things are not necessarily the people who want to. Among most hackers, he says, there is "a tinker mentality—you just want to see how it works." By taking things apart and then putting them back together, Miller learns more about products than the people who make them. Can this information be used against people?

"I'm of the mindset that anything can happen," Miller says. "There's probably nothing out there that isn't possible." That being said, however, possible and simple are not the same thing. "It's hard," Miller says. "It's totally unrealistic the way it's portrayed." He gives the example of the scene in *The Italian Job*, when a sole hacker changes the traffic lights of the city to help facilitate the getaway. "It might be possible to do what they did, but it would take like six months," Miller says. "I could imagine finding five people who could do it in six months, but one dude, especially one dude who doesn't know it like the back of his hand, no way."

The main limitation of hacking, Miller taught me, is knowledge. Every single hack is different, and no one person is familiar with all systems. For instance, when asked if it would be possible to hack a power grid, he quickly replied that yes, it would be, but he couldn't do it because he doesn't know anything about power grids. If he found an electrician to work with him, then maybe he could, but it would take him a while to learn. Specialization limits what any one person could do alone—everything is different, and everything takes a long time to understand. "No one can do all that stuff," Miller says. There is no "super-hacker" who can effortlessly and immediately break into a battery, a plane, and a computer all within an hour.

"I'm really good at what I do, but I still can't do everything. I can only do what I do—I know a few things very well," Miller explains. "If you have a Windows computer, there isn't much I can do. It doesn't mean you are secure, it just means you have to find someone else because I couldn't do it. If you have an iPhone though, you may be in trouble."

Remember the pacemaker hack mentioned earlier? Miller says that "the guy who did the pacemaker had already done an insulin pump, and it still took him a year to come up with it. This is a guy who knows embedded medical technology better than anyone, and it took him a year."

Miller stresses that hacking is hard, and is constantly getting harder. More layers of security are being added, and it is getting more and more difficult to break into hacking. That being said, he says, it is still nearly impossible to completely eliminate vulnerabilities. The trick, he says, it to make it progressively harder and harder to do—like securing a house by adding more locks and layers of protection. By making it more challenging to break in, you can force the hacker to linger longer—increasing the chances that you can catch them. Paired with the level of sophistication and computer smarts required, hacking is not something just anyone can do.

"Things are getting much harder. It's pretty hard, so the average age is going up. A twelve-year-old could write malware for sure; there is no doubt they could do that. They probably could not write a web exploit," Miller says. There are, however, exceptions to this rule. He recalls a time when—just after he told a newspaper that the days of kid hackers were over—a young hacker who goes by the name "Comex" jailbroke an iPhone. "As Comex showed, you never know," Miller says. All it really takes to be a hacker is smarts, motivation, and Internet access. No formal education or training is required. "Going to university isn't necessarily a useful option," Miller says. "There are very few programs that offer useful programs on it…maybe two in the whole country. There are not many classes out there that teach you how to write exploits, because it's hard, and not everyone can do it. Also, there aren't many professors who can do it. People who know how to do it [are the ones who] do it."

Talking to Dr. Miller helped me understand better both the possibilities, threats, and dangers of the cyber-world and the limitations in place that make cyberspace still somewhat manageable. He described a hack he did for fun in Second Life, where he was able to create a box that, when approached, would prompt a message saying "You've been hacked!" and then steal all the points from the person and give them to him. Could this be applied to banks? Yes, but not easily. There are issues with cracking the substantially more complicated defenses of the bank, and there are problems with taking a huge sum of money out without drawing suspicion—you couldn't just walk into a bank and ask for a million dollar withdrawal, he points out. It would raise eyebrows. The potential for hackers is infinite, but hacking takes sophistication and specific know-how. There is no universal code that one can hack into to control everything, nor does the ability to hack one thing necessarily translate into the ability to hack something else. It takes time, practice, and knowledge. Knowing this makes the incredible things people are able to do seem all the more incredible, and all the more real. Hacking is not magic, but a science that some people are starting to perfect.

ANONYMOUS
(IS *NOT* TRANSNATIONAL CRIMINAL ENTERPRISE)
~ CN ~

"But it is a mistake to talk of Anonymous' motives as if it were a cohesive whole. The group is a loose collection of people with different aims, involving themselves in different "operations" as they see fit. It is leaderless, it doesn't have a manifesto, it doesn't have a particular direction, nor does it go in only one direction at any one time. Given that the membership of Anonymous is based entirely on self-identification, it seems that the only real way of assessing the group as a whole is on the basis of the kinds of actions it carries out. It is essentially a banner under which hacktivists and tech-savvy individuals with a political or social agenda can rally."

– Loz Kaye[1]

THIS BOOK IS, for the most part, *not* about Anonymous—or, as a cyber-security headline summed: "Anonymous is Not your problem."

Anonymous is not a Transnational Criminal Enterprise (TCE)

or Transnational Organized Crime (TOC). Hactivism is in no way the equivalent of Organized Crime. This is a critical distinction for this book, and for cyber-understanding in general.[2]

It's important to say this because Anonymous, in popular conception, has become a Boogeyman. Because Anonymous is public, they have become synonymous with cybercrime and hacking. And because organized crime is expressly not public, all JohnQPublic sees are hactivist groups like Anonymous.

The result is that Anonymous gets the blame for much of the cybercrime in the popular press, most of which they have nothing to do with. The backlash is dangerous. The average person (which, in the cyber-world, includes most political, legal, and law enforcement officials) begins to think that, if the country forges laws to control groups like Anonymous, we will all be safe from the hacks that are draining our bank accounts, threatening our public utilities, and spying on our businesses.

In truth, if you take out hactivist groups, all of this will continue—the work of organized criminals, nation-state competition, commercial espionage, and a constantly shifting terrain of rogue actors and interest groups working for profit and power.

Organized crime groups couldn't be happier that many countries' energy and resources are going into combatting someone else. I am sure many are surprised at their good fortune that laws and security policies are focusing largely on issues that have nothing to do with them, or stopping them.

Complex, sophisticated, multi-tier, transglobal cyber-systems dedicated to illegal resource extraction and control for profit and power is the realm of transnational criminal enterprise (TCE). It thrives on invisibility and works in the shadows. Attacks into government, military, industrial, financial, and critical infrastructure depend on un-detectability. TCEs do not advertise their hacks. The parallel in the material world is the obvious fact that mafias, cartels, triads, and clandestine organizations do not advertise their exploits. Power here resides in the shadows.

While TCE is truly anonymous, Anonymous is not. The latter generally advertise their exploits. Their goal is not the kind of economic-political power that fuels TCE groups or Organized Crime syndicates. Many times it is just the opposite—to educate the public about the deeper structures of cyber-security and its relationship to political and economic power in the world. Or for the lulz, the fun, of it.[3]

TCE's goal is to break into a computing system, extract information, change data, plant malware, damage the systems they want, and then get out without being detected. Remaining undetected allows continuing entry into the compromised networks.

Anonymous has at times hacked into large industries, stolen information, called international attention to this, and then never used or sold the financial information. Their point in such cases is to show outdated and underdeveloped security practices by companies who say they are protecting their customers' personal, sensitive information.

I'm pretty certain some members of Anonymous have taken things that don't belong to them, shut down websites, and broken or broken into systems maliciously. On the other side, Anonymous hacked into several child-rape sites on the dark-net and shut them down, and assists victims in repressive regimes and war.

For people like Gene Spafford,[4] crime is crime—and battling criminal threats with illegal solutions can't be justified.

For others, hactivist groups like Anonymous are among the few successfully standing up to massive government and business practices that sacrifice citizen and consumer safety through irresponsible and, sometimes illegal, cyber-security practices. Many feel that the institutional practices allowing the theft and sale of people's most private information can be far more illicit and dangerous to citizens than the hacker's actions:

> Just for a second, let's not think about hacks as the misdeeds of anarchist computer geniuses. Let's look at them as vaccinations, helpful viruses that aid in combatting bad security practices.[5]

For example, when a November 29, 2012 post on Reddit said:

> Syria has disconnected from the Internet. All 84 of Syria's IP address blocks have become unreachable, effectively removing the country from the Internet (by Libertatea)

a response (from kadkaad) read:

> It's so interesting to see how people are waiting for "Anonymous" to do something, instead of the UN.
> Anonymous became the modern world's Internet superhero.[6]

A number of people describe Anonymous as vigilantes, simultaneously embracing both the good and bad of frontier justice without ultimate responsibility. For others, hactivists are the canary in the mine.[7] In considering the group LulzSec, Ann Smith, executive editor of *The Hacker News*, wrote:

> What I am really trying to say is that even though you can sew a thread of doing hacking for the Lulz of it, behind their actions was a real commitment to human rights. The drive and passion these people had for bringing justice to the people. I will always admire that in any form it takes place. I can excuse the nonsense and the immaturity because in the end, it really wasn't just for the Lulz of it. It really came down to being for you and me.[8]

Some, like Pierluigi Paganini, point out that anyone can be a player in an anonymous system, and because governments can engage in espionage and attacks *as* Anonymous, there may be little real incentive to shut such groups down. Paganini writes in his personal brand of English-as-a-second-language:

> Nobody really know identities of these individuals that fight for freedom and internet rights, but what is indisputable is their offensive power…Governments can masquerade their identities hacking foreign networks, they could infiltrate groups of Hacktivist acquiring sensible information, in many cases in fact following data breach the disclosed data have been used for further attacks such as APT [advanced persistent threat] and other targeted offensive.[9]

Some look at the contradictions surrounding public, political, and security reactions to hacktivism and groups like Anonymous with an eye to a larger philosophical inquiry:

- Hacktivists may engage in illegal hacking, but they are as likely to publicly expose the vulnerabilities and poor security of the places they hacked in an effort to get industry to upgrade security, to educate the public about threat structures, and to protect underdogs.
- Hacktivists may well act out of retribution, ego, and anger, but they may also seek to expose corruption and Machiavellian politics. The H.B. Gary intrusion, for example, was clearly a reaction to the company's president publicly declaring he was going to take down Anonymous. But Anonymous also posted email and company files on the Internet showing H.B. Gary's less-than-squeaky-clean business deals with government and industry.

The philosopher's question: What's the greater sin: the hacking itself, or showing the emperor has no clothes?

Endnotes

[1] Loz Kaye, "Anonymous' hactivists expose the intelligence gap," *The Guardian*, January 9, 2012, *http://www.guardian.co.uk/commentisfree/2012/jan/09/anonymous-hactivist-expose-intelligence-gap*. Accessed 1/21/2012.

[2] See: Gabriella Coleman, *Coding Freedom: The Ethics and Aesthetics of Hacking*, Princeton: Princeton University Press, 2012.

[3] Helen Walters, "Peeking Behind the curtain at Anonymous: Gabriella Coleman at TEDGlobal 2012," *TED Blog*, June 27, 2012, *http://blog.ted.com/2012/06/27/peeking-behind-the-curtain-at-anonymous-gabriella-coleman-at-tedglobal-2012/*. Accessed 5/10/13; Gabriella Coleman, "Geeks are the New Guardians of Our Civil Liberties," *MIT Technology Review*, February 4, 2013, *http://www.technologyreview.com/news/510641/geeks-are-the-new-guardians-of-our-civil-liberties/*. Accessed 5/10/13; Gabriella Coleman, "Am I Anonymous?" *Limn*, #2, *http://limn.it/am-i-anonymous/*. Accessed 5/10/13.

[4] Personal communication, June 2012.

[5] Joshua Kopstein, "Dear Big Companies: Getting Hacked Is Good for You," *Motherboard*, June 8, 2011, *http://motherboard.vice.com/2011/6/8/dear-big-companies-getting-hacked-is-good-for-you*. Accessed 12/4/2011.

[6] *Reddit*, technology, comments, *http://www.reddit.com/r/technology/comments/13zsqr/syria_has_disconnected_from_the_internet_all84/c78mie1*. Accessed 11/29/2012.

[7] Gabriella Coleman, "Hacker Politics and Publics," *Public Culture* 23:3, 2011:511.

[8] Ann Smith, "For the Lutz of It, I Apologize to Lulzsec," *The Hacker News*, August 2012, Issue 13:8, *www.thehackernews.com*.

[9] Pierluigi Paganini, *The Deep Dark Web: The Hidden World*, Naples, Italy: Paganini/Amores Publishing, 2012:83.

Mark Interview
Teenager – Gamer
December 14, 2012
~ CN ~

THIS IS THE FIRST TIME a young generation has the will to change, has the power to change. In a way, with the advent of the Internet culture, everybody has the same amount of power.

Change what? It's complicated. Not the world per se. We're not going to change the structure of government and the way people see each other. What we can do is humanize each other. In the past, a person in America and a person in China almost didn't think of each other as being in the same world. But now we can video-chat, play a game together, connect in seconds—we can see each other as a shared society.

So imagine there is a kid in China or Iran or Syria and another country declares war with their country, not necessarily America, but America is a country expected to declare war. That kid can go down into his basement and talk to his friends in other countries— and I can assure you that none of them want the war. In talking, they humanize each other. And it will get harder and harder for a formal conflict or war or international dispute to be taken seriously, because it will be like two big heads (governments) talking to each other, and the bodies (us) are getting along.

Right now there is the war between regulation and the creative side. At the moment it seems like the creative side people are the underdogs. To those on the creative side, everyone is seen more as humans, as the other people in our community—communities that are changing, that are no longer geographic units, but are changing into networks. You can't really look at it on a geographic scale because, if you tried to map the realities of these new network communities—like a globe divided by colored territories and borders—each person and each household will be a different color. People link up, they belong, all over the geographic map.

It almost forces an open-mindedness and a discussion. The destructive, however, does pose a real threat. Someone can get online and hack into someone else's database and re-write it, or launch a missile. More important, though, is that there is a greater community building networks of relationships across distances, not only internationally, but also among the more oppressed groups.

Look at the mayor of Reykjavik, Iceland. He's an anarchist and he is a self-proclaimed nerd, geek. He dresses up his family in Star-War clothes and takes pictures. His ideal is for everyone to be demilitarized and for Iceland to be a demilitarized zone where people and heads of countries can come to resolve conflicts. His ideas are the ideal of Internet culture in many ways.

The thing is, my generation, the studies are saying, is very similar to the online cultures I'm describing here—and the older ways are dying out. This stands against the status quo of the world's powers, both in business and politics. Minorities, silent majorities, will be able to build themselves over time.

In terms of the constructive aspects of the Internet communities, I feel like, at some level, we won't let [societal] collapse happen. The governments may be sending armies and destroying each other—but, no matter what, there will be people out there rebuilding. Take Syria for example. When the government cut off the Internet, people around the world sent dial-up codes and other support so the people in Syria could communicate what was going on and how to help—and people did.

I feel this will happen in any war or collapse or problem. I think my generation sees pretty clearly the serious problems in the world, and what can come from these. The key value emerging in the Internet generations is: stop following the formal system that has been universally accepted and create your own.

So the online community changes interactions in the real world by changing the way relationships are defined, because you can make anything "not limited." It's more about keeping the world on the right course—rather than on one heading towards a collapse—because, in reality, the collapse is irrelevant. Because things will keep going on around—and much of the Internet and gaming community has withdrawn itself from the part of the community in threat of collapse. They'll keep going, their world will keep turning, even if the rest of the world doesn't.

Darknets

~ CN ~

"It seems likely that the internet will remain in its Gold Rush phase for some time yet. And in the crevices and corners of its slightly thrown-together structures, darknets and other private online environments will continue to flourish. They can be inspiring places to spend time in, full of dissidents and eccentrics and the internet's original freewheeling spirit. But a darknet is not always somewhere for the squeamish."

— Andy Beckett[1]

There are vast stretches of cyber-landscape Google and its sister search engines can't find. Darknet, invisible web, Deepnet, un-indexed net, dark address space—these uncharted realms of the Internet have generated numerous names. At the most basic level,

> Darknets exploit the infrastructure of the Internet but stand apart from it. They use non-standard protocols and ports to create secure networks for groups of all kinds, from dissidents to illegal file sharers, and from terrorists to anti-terrorists.[2]

These terms all refer to websites on the Internet that public search engines like Google, Bing, and Yahoo are unable to index, and thus report in a search.

> And yet, in a sense, they are all part of the same picture: beyond the confines of most people's online lives, there is a vast other internet out there, used by millions but largely ignored by the media and properly understood by only a few computer scientists.[3]

No one knows for certain how large these areas of the Internet are, though all agree the deep-net is far larger than the known—the surface or superficial web—indexed by Google. Michael Bergman published the classic study of the invisible net in 2001.[4] He pointed out that the very boundaries of what the web *is* are increasingly blurred. Because of this, "You can't talk about how big the internet is. Because what is the metric?"

Given this, Bergman estimates the dark-net is 400-550 times larger than the commonly defined surface World Wide Web. Internet searches are searching only 0.03% of the total web-pages available. The deep web, he found, is the fastest growing category of new information on the Internet.

Over a decade later, cyber-specialists continue to affirm the incalculable nature of the invisible net, and most cite Bergman's figures on the size of the Darknet as the best estimates to date. Virtually all agree with his assessment that the value of Deep Web content is immeasurable.[5]

Beyond this consensus, people agree on little else. Descriptions are as varied as the six blind men describing an elephant. The *reason* a person enters into the dark-net often provides the *definition* they give it.

- People supporting political and religious freedom herald the deep-net as one of the few potentially safe places persecuted dissidents living under repressive governments can find expression and communicate globally.

• For those interested in the illicit, the immoral, and the perverse, the dark-net is the haunt of pedophiles, counterfeiters, drug pushers, violent pornography, assassins for hire, and other shadowy figures of the netherworld.

• Militaries and governments rely on the invisible net to protect their data and computing systems. The US military's Secret Internet Protocol Router Network (SIPRNet), for example, uses internet protocols (TCP/IP, http etc.), but is air-gapped—secured by maintaining actual physical space from computing devices and software linking externally—from the public Internet.

• Digital-intruders troll sites selling botnet software, intrusion malware, anti-virus evasion products, hacking-as-a-service, stolen data, and legal services if one gets caught.

• People can hunt for legal car sales, a special antique, databases of cat lovers, and musicians producing cutting-edge music. For example, Juliana Freire at the University of Utah leads a deep-web search project called "Deep Peep."

• Consumers find smorgasbords of extra-legal commodities and services from fake legal documents and identities, through pharmaceuticals and piracy stock-exchanges, to trafficked minors and cyber-weapons.

• Media moguls fret excessively about sites dedicated to free music, movie, and copyrighted file sharing.

• Smugglers can download forged government Customs forms for bringing goods into a country.

• It is, in a manner of speaking, a home, or at least an oasis, to groups like the FreeNet Project, dedicated to the founding computer principles of open access, freedom of speech, and self-regulation.

• And dedicated librarians produce exceptional search engines to find scholarly, technical, and professional publications not directly accessible by Google. They seek to put information on any medical topic, legal question, food interest, environmental issue, policy issue, educational development, great literature—ad infinitum—at the reader's fingertips.

Complicating the issue even further, as Michael Bergman demonstrated over a decade ago, determining with any accuracy what and where the boundaries of the Net are proves nigh on impossible. Different realms of invisible and surface nets variously interpenetrate, merge, mingle, and break apart—both on purpose and unwittingly.

> A spokesman for the Police Central e-crime Unit [PCeU] at the Metropolitan Police points out that many internet secrets hide in plain sight: "A lot of internet criminal activity is on online forums that are not hidden, you just have to know where to find them. Like paedophile websites: people who use them might go to an innocent-looking website with a picture of flowers, click on the 18th flower, arrive on another innocent-looking website, click on something there, and so on."[6]

In a similar vein, Beckett adds, a recently busted paedophile ring met on Facebook.

At the other end of the spectrum:

> While a "darknet" is an online network such as Freenet that is concealed from non-users, with all the potential for transgressive behavior that implies, much of "the deep web," spooky as it sounds, consists of unremarkable consumer and research data that is beyond the reach of search engines.
>
> "Dark address space" often refers to internet addresses that, for purely technical reasons, have simply stopped working.[7]

These sites that have been abandoned, forgotten, and lost through decades of millions of users are "hot property" to some, who troll online looking for such places.

"In 2000 dark and murky address space was a bit of a novelty," says Labovitz [chief scientist at Arbor Networks, a leading online security firm]. "This is now an entrenched part of the daily life of the internet." Defunct online companies; technical errors and failures; disputes between internet service providers; abandoned addresses once used by the US military in the earliest days of the internet—all these have left the online landscape scattered with derelict or forgotten properties, perfect for illicit exploitation, sometimes for only a few seconds before they are returned to disuse. How easy is it to take over a dark address? "I don't think my mother could do it," says Labovitz. "But it just takes a PC and a connection. The internet has been largely built on trust."[8]

Once found, they may be used for a matter of seconds or minutes only—sending untraceable commands and data.

Given this Internet complexity, a new threat horizon has emerged. An untold number of supposedly closed and secure sites have, by the simplest of human errors—like plugging one cable into the wrong socket or some software oversights—opened a door to Net access, thereby mingling hidden and public spaces, often in unknown and dangerous ways.

John Matherly created a search engine he dubbed Shodan to map and capture the specifications of everything linked to the Internet, from computers and printers to industrial communications equipment and web servers. As *The Washington Post* wrote:

> He had no inkling it was about to alter the balance of security in cyberspace.[9]

Shodan, which can be accessed by any interested person, has gathered data on hundreds of millions of devices, detailing their locations and operating systems. Startling data began to emerge: one researcher found a nuclear particle accelerator at the University of California Berkeley linked to the Internet with little to no security.

Eireann Leverett made headlines when he used Shodan to identify over 10,000 computers used to control industrial equipment and infrastructure that were Net-connected, many with vulnerabilities. And worse, many operators did not know the extent of their online exposure, or even that their machines were online. Leverett warned that malicious actors might well be identifying and targeting vulnerable systems in the same way.

Something of a Shodan research subculture has formed, with people like Billy Rios (Google) and Terry McCorkle (Boeing) saying their studies suggest the situation is even worse than Leverett finds. As O'Harrow Jr. explains:

> Because of the strange nature of cyberspace, even an employee passing through a plant with a wireless connection on a laptop can create a temporary data link that exposes control systems to intruders.
>
> "They have sort of connected through osmosis," said Marty Edwards, a senior cyber-security official at the Department of Homeland Security. "What we have done is connect to everything."[10]

Anything that is invisible to the public world is ripe for myth, fear, magic, and power-mongering. " 'The darkweb'; 'the deep web'; 'beneath the surface web'—the metaphors alone make the Internet feel suddenly more unfathomable and mysterious."[11]

Many who write on the Darknet in the public media are fixated on the sites breaking moral taboos, some in horrifying ways. But the Net, like the humans who create it, can fall prey to the mythical Coyote: the world's Trickster. It never gives you quite what you expect.

The many realms of the invisible net underscore the important fact that there is no one, single darknet, no integrated deep web. Steve Mansfield-Devine writes that there isn't one big darknet—that it contains "an enormous array of different networks and actors." In terms of crime alone, he cites Eli Jellenc's (iDefense, international cyber-intelligence) estimates that there are 1,000-5,000 important criminal darknets globally, and that these are constantly changing. Because these often break down by language groups, Mansfield-Devine says, one can't speak of an overarching, truly interconnected global criminal-web.[12]

At the same time many scientists prefer not to put breakthrough work on hack-able cloud servers and places like Google Docs where the companies own this data in some important legal ways. As well, "Tor's users, according to its website, include US secret service 'field agents' and 'law enforcement officers.' "[13]

The fact that the invisible-net hosts both secure scientific sites and criminal ones is just one of the Net's fundamental ironies. In the final sum, Beckett reminds us, the Darknet and its main navigation software TOR

> [I]s used both by the American state and by some of its fiercest opponents. On the hidden internet, political life can be as labyrinthine as in a novel by Thomas Pynchon.

And he asks: "Does it represent the future of life online or the past?"

Endnotes

[1] Andy Beckett, "The dark side of the internet," *The Guardian*, November 26, 2009, *http://www.theguardian.com/technology/2009/nov/26/dark-side-internet-freenet*. Accessed 3/27/2012.

[2] Steve Mansfield-Devine, "Going over to the dark side," *http://www.web-vivant.com/feature-darkents.html*. Accessed 12/16/11.

[3] Beckett, op. cit.

[4] Michael Bergman, "The Deep Web: Surfacing Hidden Value," *The Journal of Electronic Publishing* 7(1), 2001.

[5] Beckett, op. cit.

[6] ibid.

[7] ibid.

[8] ibid.

[9] Robert O'Harrow Jr., "Cyber search engine Shodan exposes industrial control systems to new risks," *The Washington Post,* June 3, 2012, *http://www.washingtonpost.com/investigation/cyber-search-engine*. Accessed 6/27/12.

[10] ibid.

[11] Beckett, op. cit.

[12] Mansfield-Devine, op. cit. Accessed 12/16/11.

[13] Beckett, op. cit.

— Part Three —

Digital Criminals and Shadow-Lands

CYBER-CRIMINALS
~ CN ~

"IT'S A GREAT TIME TO BE A CYBERCRIMINAL."
— GRAGIDO, MOLINA, PIRC, SELBY[1]

"WE KNOW ONE OR TWO THINGS ABOUT HACKERS FOR
SURE. ONE IS THAT 95 PERCENT OF THEM ARE MALE,
WHICH TELLS YOU A GREAT DEAL IN ITSELF. THE OTHER IS
THAT HACKERS, UNLIKE PEOPLE INVOLVED IN TRADITIONAL
ORGANIZED CRIME, IF WE'RE TALKING ABOUT CRIMINAL
HACKERS, …DON'T NEED TO DEPLOY VIOLENCE TO GET
INTO THE GAME. YOU DON'T NEED A BASEBALL BAT TO
HACK, WHICH IS FOR ME VERY IMPORTANT BECAUSE IT
ATTRACTS A DIFFERENT TYPE OF CHARACTER."
— MISHA GLENNY[2]

"THE PHRASE 'TRANSNATIONAL CRIMINAL ENTERPRISES'
WAS CRAFTED IN RECENT YEARS TO REPLACE THE TRADI-
TIONAL TAG, 'ORGANIZED CRIME.' WHILE A DECADE AGO,
ORGANIZED CRIME GROUPS HIRED HACKERS TO COMPRO-
MISE COMPUTERS AND STEAL DATA, TODAY HACKERS HAVE
FORMED THEIR OWN GLOBAL GROUPS AND UNDERGROUND
NETWORKS AND WORK INDEPENDENTLY OF THE TRADI-
TIONAL ORGANIZED CRIME GROUPS. THE PRIMARY MOTIVE
OF THESE GLOBAL CRIMINAL ENTERPRISES: SHEER PROFIT."
— PwC[3]

IN MEDICINE, you focus on the most serious threat, working your way down to the less dangerous illnesses only after you successfully treat the first. You don't treat a cold before setting a broken bone.

This does not seem to apply with the same gravity in the emerging field of cyber-security. As Gragido et. al. sum up, Internet users are "Locking the doors while opening the windows: Inviting the cybercriminals into our world and our lives."[4]

A large portion of the *public* media discussion around cyber-security laws revolves around controlling illegal media, and intrusions for immediate financial gain—the proverbial music & movie, credit card, and identity theft heists. The criminal in most of these public discussions is portrayed as your run-of-the-mill thief who in the 20th century would be stealing albums in a store by stuffing them in his or her bag, or is cat-burglar-ing your home or business—and has moved on to digital theft in the 21st century.

Far more rarely does the discussion turn to sophisticated networks of professionals who break into RSA's networks to steal the security tokens that make the Internet possible, and then use the tokens to break into Lockheed Martin's computers for military defense data; or the organized criminal systems that set up state-of-the-art botnets throughout the banking industry to skim off millions from target institutions; or the people who hacked into a couple of satellites in space, or military drones in Afghanistan.

I want to underscore the words "public media" above, for inversely, these topics are the meat of cyber-security and techno-savvy blogs and news sites. Here, assessments tend to embrace a different logic:

> Why do in-house cyber security people, processes, and technology often fail to detect advanced cyber threats designed to maintain remote-access for as long as possible? One reason: The cyber threat landscape is

organized, global, highly motivated, sometimes well-funded, patient, and fully immersed in the tradecraft.[5]

By law, all these acts—from stealing a credit card number to emptying bank vaults—are illegal. But they are illegal in the same way that colds and cancer are all diseases. Not all illnesses or crimes are equal. As yet, few objective considerations of hierarchies of harm exist for digital crime.[6]

> In *Neuromancer*, Gibson says, "The future is already here. It's just unevenly distributed." Drug cartels are using robotic submarines to deliver narcotics. Criminal groups are already using robotics, criminals are using artificial intelligence when they're scripting computer viruses. There are massive portions of our global Internet compromised and botnet armies do exist. So the future is already here, whether or not people recognize the fact that there are people with ill intentions, people with intentions to massively harm others that are exploiting robotics, artificial intelligence and synthetic biology. That's here.[7]

Gragido and Pirc write to this future, introducing what they define as the next generation of cybercrime: Subversive Multivector Threat (SMT). This involves the convergence of threat vectors, including those once exclusive to defense, intelligence, and law enforcement; state-sponsored and economic espionage; complex criminal organizations; and opportunistic ventures.

SMTs are more comprehensive than Advanced Persistent Threats [APTs] recognized today, and they are by definition subversive (against political, industrial, financial, or socio-moral systems) and multivector (employing multiple pathways to goal). This convergence is complicated and intensified by global interconnectivity, and by the "butterfly effect" of chaos theory.

For Gragido and Pirc, SMTs represent a paradigm-shifting development. As such, the authors conclude that gaining an understanding of the organizations employing SMTs (from criminal to state-sponsored), the emerging trends characterizing these threats, and the economic ecosystems that support SMTs is critical. While there is, they note, little understanding of the sophistication of cybercriminals so far, there is a worrying amount of mal-information.

To date, comprehensive analyses of the global patterns and trends of digital crime across the world's populations remain elusive. This is in part due to the fact that much of digital crime goes unreported, either because the targets don't want to admit their vulnerabilities, or because they don't know they've suffered intrusions. Perhaps in some cases people are hesitant to provide data that could confirm Joseph Menn's unsettling observation that in the cyber-world:

> Crime pays very, very well, and in the big picture, their ecosystem is better than ours. They do capitalism better than we do. They specialize to a great extent. They reinvest in R&D."[8]

The allure of information ushers in a new era in theft, whether for espionage, profit, war, or social control. This rests in the simple fact that, while stealing material goods is obvious to the victim and to investigators—the goods are no longer there; stealing information can be utterly invisible to the victims—an intruder merely makes a copy of the data, leaving the original intact.

This one fact changes the fundamental definition of "value" that has been operating since the dawn of markets.

Information is a quintessentially renewable resource; it can be taken an unlimited number of times without losing or diluting the source, and it can be sold and resold without anyone giving the resource away. It need not be transferred from one to another, just cloned and shared.

Since economic value for both legal and illegal commodities has largely been assessed throughout history on "limited" goods (to possess a good by definition means no one else does), the introduction of "unlimited goods" (unlimited copies of equal quality can be made, exchanged, and owned by multiple people) presages a radical shift in economic valuation.

Assessments of digital extra-legality would help provide tools to shed light on emergent terrains of a globalizing cyber-integrated world:

- Who are the key targets, and what constitutes value in the criminal cyber/espionage world?
- How much of the intrusions and information theft from government, industry, and finance is done by criminal organizations in the pursuit of profit, and how much by nation-states engaging in espionage; and where are, and aren't, linkages among these groups?
- Exactly "what" is being stolen? How much is lost to "low hanging fruit crime" (credit card and identity theft, spam-Gen2, etc.) versus highly organized financial and information extractions?
- What percentages are theft, changing or damaging data, controlling or damaging systems, or using zombie-systems as middle-men in more extensive attacks?
- Who profits, and where are the profits going; how are they laundered?

And the larger questions in the intersections of digital extra-legality with the world-in-progress:

- How are classical economies shaped and changed by these actions and valuations?

- How are political processes affected?
- What constitutes power in digital landscapes?

In what cyber-communities often refer to as FUD—fear, uncertainty, and doubt—answers to these kinds of questions are frequently laced with emotionalism, sensationalism, ulterior motives, misinformation, and manipulation. At a more basic level:

> There is currently no globally accepted definition of cybercrime. Therefore, organizations don't know about the danger, which means it's harder to detect and fight it. Essentially, if the "concept of the enemy" is blurred, any efforts to fight it might prove futile.[9]

Contradictions thus abound. For example, industrial cyber-theft is often attributed to espionage by Chinese government-affiliated groups. Saber-rattling is fairly common in US-based discussions of this.

In addition, while most agree that China is certainly a major force in cyber-espionage, those who are working to assess global patterns for nation-state involvement in "cyber-politics" write that over a hundred of the world's countries are developing cyber-espionage and cyber-warfare capacities.

At the same time, discussions of organized cyber-crime networks circulate widely—such as Goodman's observation that 85% of data stolen is taken by organized crime:[10]

> Cybercrime is already an agile, globalized and outsourced business. "Anything that would motivate a startup employee would motivate a criminal," explains Goodman. "They want money, they want shares in the business, they want a challenge, they don't want a 9-5 environment. They want respect of their peers, and they are engaged in a game of us against them."[11]

Without a more nuanced understanding of global-threat eco-systems, I, like many, am left wondering which "truths" of cyber in-security are objective representations and which are the results of FUD, vested interests, or poor research. In this vacuum of objectivity, the tendency of political and public media to frame discussions of cyber-powers in out-dated 20th-century, politico-military terms and ideologies (Cold War competition, Hot War sovereign battles) could inadvertently spark dangerously real conflict.

Endnotes

[1] Will Gragido, Daniel Molina, John Pirc and Nick Selby, *Blackhatonomics: An Inside Look at the Economics of Cybercrime*, Waltham, MA: Elsevier Press, 2013:2.

[2] Misha Glenny, quoted in Warren Hoge, "Interview with Misha Glenny, Cybercrime Expert," 2/13/2012, *http://www.theglobalobservatory.org/ interviews/213-interview-with-misha-glenny-cybercrime-expert.html*. Accessed 4/2/2012.

[3] PwC, "Are you compromised but don't know it?: A new philosophy for cyber security," January 2011:6, *www.pwc.com/us/en/forensic-services/publications/ are-you-compromised.jhtml*.

[4] Gragido, Molina, Pirc and Selby, op. cit., 121.

[5] PwC, op. cit., 7.

[6] Franz-Stefan Gady suggests we need the equivalent to the U.S. Center for Disease Control and Prevention for cyber-crime. "Statistics and the 'Cyber Crime Epidemic,'" *Huffington Post Tech*, September 22, 2011, *http://www. huffingtonpost.com/franzstefan-gady/cybercrime-statistics_b_974005.html*. Accessed 12/2/2011.

[7] Ben Lillie and Marc Goodman, "How much should we worry about future crimes? A Q&A with Marc Goodman," *Ted Blog*, August 03, 2012, *http://blog. ted.com/2012/08/03/how-much-should-we-worry-about-future-crimes-a-qa-with-marc-goodman/*. Accessed 12/8/2012.

[8] Dana Gardner, "The Cyber-Crime Landscape," *BriefingsDirect* interview with Joseph Menn by Dana Gardner, *http://soa.sys-con/node/2116303/print.* Accessed February 5, 2012.

[9] PwC, "Cybercrime: Protecting Against the Growing Threat—Global Economic Crime Survey," November, 2011, *www.pwc.com/crimesurvey.*

[10] seofacts, "Big Data, Big Attraction for Organized Crime," *http://www.seofacts.biz/big-data-big-attraction-for-organized-crime.*

[11] Ciara Byrne, "Crimesourcing and how data criminals are like startup employees," 9/23/11, *http://venturebeat.com/2011/09/23/.* Accessed 2/5/12.

Brian Krebs Interview
KrebsOnSecurity.com
December 2012 & October 2013

- CN -

THE AVERAGE CRIME FORUM is very stratified, and there is a considerable amount of intelligence one can gain from lurking on the underground—both on closed, private sites and open ones, like insidepro.com, a password-cracking forum. Here, for example, you can find massive caches of stolen hashed passwords—the people putting them there want the community to help crack the hashes.

There is a lot of activity on these sites from both sides. "White hats" are getting into these forums and seeing what's up, what's going on. Many times people figure out the source of a previous attack this way—where the data came from, what company or site was broached, who were the victims, what data was taken. A company or government site all too often finds out intruders got into their systems and stole data because someone saw their private information in these dumps.

Further down on the underground, it becomes more difficult to get into these sites. The people in these places have to trust that the rest of the members are criminals and not law enforcement. To gain access, people have to be vouched for; they may have to give a deposit of one to two thousand dollars, or more. There is a vetting period where members ask newcomers questions: what have you done, what's your CV—that kind of thing. How a person answers the questions—who they know and what they've done—is considered, and then the members vote on whether to let the person in.

You tend to find stratification on the criminal sites. For example, there may be sub-forums for spam, money-laundering, money mules, cashing out information. Of course there are places to buy any kind of malware kits, and links to purchase any of the services for cybercrimes a person may not know how to commit themselves—from code-writing and anti-virus evasion to selling off the bounty from a successful break-in.

I see the same guys moderating the same sub-forums across different sites. Watching this over time, it makes sense. These guys have extensive resources; they know everyone in the business; they've written the key malware; and they've developed the infrastructure of the underground sites, groups, and economies.

I'd estimate that just a few guys—maybe around 100—are running a majority of the financial cyber-crime forums; in the final count at the top levels, it's not a lot of people. That said, there are tens of thousands of ankle-biters, mostly teenagers, involved.

This is a cash-rich economy—one that deals in cars, computers, women, drugs. This is an important point; the economy we're talking of here is a cash economy. There are lots of parallels to the drug world. In fact, many started out peddling porn and drugs.

Most forums will at one point or another let noobie/newbie or inexperienced hackers in, even when many of them turn out to young and reckless. The reason is that the newbies are some of the most active buyers on the forums, and the guys running the forums are usually the ones selling products and services. Any cyber-crime organization has already been turn-keyed. These kinds of people make the forums go around; the new users who do stupid stuff—rip people off—get banned and kicked off pretty quickly.

With enough time and resources, a patient, talented attacker can break into just about anything. It's why groups like Anonymous are successful. They have lots of time and determination. Their chief weapon is social engineering. Virtually every system is vulnerable to social engineering. A 17-year-old in their basement has time. The attacks by the Chinese are not too different.

Russians and Brazilians are doing cyber-crime for different reasons than the Chinese. The Chinese take a long view of everything—5, 10, 15, 20 years down the road. They consider: How do these resources help our business expand and grow? What does this mean for our future? How do we get a better bargaining chip at the table in negotiating contracts for work in China and for the country's business?

The Russians are more opportunistic. They employ shotgun attacks and see what sticks, and what they have. Then they take a closer look to see which resources have the best short-term value. They may even sell off resources that they don't have time or inclination to monetize.

Sometimes, the financially oriented attackers are not so aware of the strategic value of the victim systems they've hacked. I've seen such groups compromise systems in a bank and treat them as nothing more than another infected desktop; whereas, if they took a closer look at the Internet address of the infected system, they'd probably use that resource differently. What I worry about is the financially-oriented attackers doing a better job of understanding what they have—that they're inside of X number of banks and Fortune 500 companies with their various botnets—the intersection of espionage and commerce.

On the subject of cybercrime, there's lot of hype in the media. Even the tech-oriented publications take the most interesting stories and amplify them. The problem is that there's so much hyperbole, it's hard to know what to focus on and what to take seriously. That's why I focus on the new developments and their direct impact.

They say "you're one paycheck away from the street." Well, every organization is one zero-day away from the street. I'm not the author of that, but this is what needs to be the starting point of our work. This fact shouldn't be shocking.

People need to recognize the importance of listening to the underground. You see people trading zero-days. There was a forum I stumbled on the other day that had an unpatched zero-day / Flash volume. This is Huge. Ninety percent of computer users are using this! And this was selling for $100,000 on the underground— $100,000 to have potential access to 90% of all computers in use. There is always a zero-day out there for the software you're using.

There is a lot of media attention paid to zero-day vulnerabilities, but most companies should not spend too much of their resources and money defending against these threats, which are hard to do much about anyway. Instead, most organizations are better off locking down their systems to protect against the most common attacks and network/system vulnerabilities and misconfigurations that allow a majority of the successful intrusions.

Cybercrime is an attractive profession because the chances of getting caught and being put in jail are relatively small, compared to other types of crimes. Probably only one-tenth of 1% of those involved in cybercrime get even a scare from law enforcement. There is a lot of easy money to be made. Cybercrime persists because there are seldom any consequences.

You've heard the saying, "Evil flourishes when good people do nothing." You can insert cybercrime in that phrase. The examples are everywhere—from when a bank gets hit, $600,000 lost by a customer, and the bank fails to notify all the appropriate people.

This is a real problem for everyone. People all too often say, "I don't have sensitive data. This isn't a work computer. Who would be interested in me? Why does it matter; what's the big deal?" I hear this quite a bit, even from people who should know better. Check the graphic on my website for the list of myriad uses for a hacked PC. People may think: It's *just* a computer; I just check my email and surf a bit. Who can get anything from that? But they don't get the fact that once it's hacked, *it's not your computer anymore.*

Botnets

~ CN ~

"So the way the Internet is being used now is in very, very grave trouble and not reliable. If they turned all the botnets in the world on a given target, that target is gone."

— Joseph Menn[1]

"We're beginning to see about 4 million new botnet infections every month....It's a moving target."

— Howard Schmidt[2]

How would you react if you found out that someone covertly installed spying equipment in your home that was recording your conversations, videotaping your activities, monitoring your financial transactions down to collecting your account passwords, logging your purchases, copying all your emails and Internet use, recording your phone calls and texts, tracking your GPS locations, and stealing your address books and contact lists to do the same to your friends, family, colleagues, and associates?

What if you found out further that the people who had installed the spying system in your home were renting out this surveillance system into your life for as little as $10.00 an hour on websites; and, in some instances, selling all the information they gather about you on clandestine websites to people who variously want to steal your identity, blackmail you, use your credit cards, drain your bank account, steal your work, or gain access to classified information you have?

Or that they were using your home as a staging ground for illegal activities without your knowledge—running anything from counterfeit medicines to codes for attacking a country's critical infrastructure through your address?

There's a decent chance that any or all of this actually could happen—about a 10 to 20 percent chance, according to botnet specialists. Some place the odds even higher.

One in five households contain botnet-infected devices (which can include computers, smartphones, and tablets) botnet expert Gunter Ollmann estimated for 2012.[3] In terms of home computers alone, around 10 to 15 percent are infected with botnet crime-ware. These figures hold both across the U.S.A. and internationally.[4] Some countries are hit even harder: in the previous year, 2011, around 20% of all broadband subscribers in Israel and Greece appeared to be recruited regularly into a botnet on their computers alone.[5] The study didn't include other infected devices like smartphones. Infection rates have continued to increase globally at a dangerous rate. To complicate matters further, approximately 40 percent of infected devices have two or more different botnet infections on them, according to botnet security company Damballa.

For large enterprise networks (as distinct from residential systems), Ollmann writes that in 2012 Damballa found, on average, between three to seven percent of assets within enterprise networks were infected and actively searching for, or successfully connecting with, a cyber-criminal's C&C (Command & Control) server.

"An example of how easy it is to build a simple botnet is a new construction kit called TwitterNET Builder. All the budding botmaster needs to do is enter the name of a Twitter account that infected machines must monitor for commands, and then press a button. The software creates a custom executable. The botmaster then sends the executable to victims to infect themselves."

— Jon Thompson[6] (Note: This was written in 2010, in the adolescence of botnet development.)

Bots & Botmasters today can:

1) own your machine.

They can install their own operating system, preempting yours—giving them access to everything that you have on, and do, with your computer or smartphone. Alfred Huger, Vice President of engineering at Immunet, noted that, by spring 2010, their data showed that seven out of ten threats they collected had the ability to download software allowing them full central control of the bots. This was before the advent of widely available DIY (Do It Yourself) botnet kits—ZeuS and SpyEye, for example, being recent classics.[7]

2) infect your machine without your making a "click-error."

Sophisticated crime-ware can be delivered "drive-by"—inserted on legitimate sites like news, sports, dictionaries, and charities without their knowledge. As of 2012, SophosLabs reported 30,000 websites were infected *every day*, and 80% of the infected sites are legitimate. In fact, 85% of all malware found comes from the Web.[8] In addition, intruders can gain access through vulnerabilities in Bluetooth, wireless, and public networks (like hotels), and by infected accessories (like jump drives).

3) avoid detection—by law enforcement, anti-virus, and competing botnets.

For example, by 2009-2010, one of the earlier "un-killable" botnets, TDL-4 (also known as TDSS and Alureon), infects the system's master boot record (MBR) that boots the entire system, so that the malware is loaded before the operating system and, upon installation, removes other competing bot-malware already operating in the victim's device.[9]

By 2012, Jonathan Brossard showed that he could flash the BIOS of computers *before* they were purchased, say in transit from factories, giving him complete control of the devices. As the BIOS are fundamental to computer operation, there is no way to remove or clean an infected device. As Brossard told me: "The only thing you can do to get rid of a BIOS hack is throw away the machine." Brossard found that his code worked with 230 different motherboards—allowing him access to a wide range of machines.[10]

4) act like people.

Automated social-bots and chat-bots troll social media sites like Facebook and Twitter acting like your friend. Many reading this now are likely engaged in ongoing online conversations with "people" you like that are, in fact, nothing more than clever chunks of code. As you chat about your day, these bot-friends are delving into your private information, practicing the art of social manipulation, and possibly disseminating misinformation, propaganda, and political smear-campaigns.

The outcome is well-captured in the title "The Socialbot Network: When Bots Socialize for Fame and Money."[11] Boshmaf and his colleagues at the University of British Columbia found that Online Social Networks, such as Facebook, can be infiltrated with a success rate of up to 80%.

5) avoid take-down.

The better malware today uses peer-to-peer (P2P) technology to communicate with (and infect) other machines in the botnet without relying on the central Command and Control server(s). Traditionally, most take-downs by law enforcement and security specialists worked by taking over the centralized C&C server(s) controlling the botnet (e.g. Coreflood, Rustock, Waledac 1.0 & 2.0).

With P2P technology, taking down the C&C server doesn't kill the system; therefore, botnet owners can retain control of their net even if infected machines can't reach the servers.[12]

Worse still, there may be no sure-fire way to kill a botnet. "Zombie" (slang for bot) captures this meaning as well: a Zombie is already dead so killing it is essentially meaningless. All any zombie-master has to do is reactivate the infection codes and the zombie walks again.

Even after a botnet is taken down, it is notoriously difficult to remove the malware from the victim's computers—which may be spread across the globe. This malware can be re-accessed by a botmaster from another computer or smartphone and fresh software programs. For example, on March 28, 2012, Kaspersky Lab, Crowdstrike, Dell SecureWorks, and Honeynet Project announced taking control of the 1,110,000-strong Kelihos botnet. One day later, the Kelihos gang had already begun building a new botnet—"paying creators of a Facebook worm to install their Trojan horse on already-infected computers" (compromising over 70,000 accounts that day), and leveraging the worm to regain control of the Kelihos bots sinkholed by Kaspersky and partners with their new

Kelihos version. A year later, FireEye reported that, on Feburary 11, 2013, the Kelihos botnet was back in action—again.[13]

Answers are not getting any easier. In early June 2013, Microsoft and the FBI reported "taking down" the Citadel botnet. More than 5 million people in 90 countries were infected by this malware, and more than $500 million in assets were stolen in attacks targeting banks primarily in the US, Australia, and Italy. A bare week later, John Leyden reported: "Zombies just won't stay underground," adding: "the zombie network is already rising from the grave again."[14]

6) defend themselves.

Some botnets are able to detect and react to attempts to study them—at times demonstrating the ability to attack those doing the studying.[15]

7) adapt quickly to our evolving world.

Within two weeks of each other, security researchers Gabriel Menezes Nuñes and Luigi Auriemma both discovered ways to remotely send code to a television. Auriemma explains that if the TV is connected to the Internet and has an IP address, but doesn't have the appropriate filters, an attack over the Internet is possible. Dan Goodin sums this up:

> TV-based botnets? DoS attacks on your fridge? More plausible than you think.[16]

ANATOMY OF A ZOMBIE:

> *"Ten years ago the first malicious bot was discovered, and five years ago only the most initiated would have heard of botnets.*
>
> *"Botnets are here to stay, and with broadband infrastructure being brought to more regions of Africa and Asia bringing more of their populations online, the potential for further increase in their size and exploitation capabilities is vast. If botnets are capable of taking out a small first-world country today, it is very worrying to consider what they might be capable of in the future."*
>
> *– Claire Elliott[17]*

You hear about a breaking news story, an earthquake or maybe a movie-star escapade, and go online to check it out. Nestled covertly on a legitimate news-story (or sports, weather, pornography, celebrity gossip, ad infinitum) website is a piece of malware—an iFrame—so small it can hide in a single pixel.

A small piece of code moves into your computer. You have no idea you were hit in this drive-by. Its job is to "call home"; that is, to call a Command and Control (C&C) computer, smartphone, or tablet anywhere on earth that has an Internet connection. This surreptitiously opens a backdoor for the C&C server to send and install whatever programs they want onto your machine. It's a bit like the person in the vampire movie who opens the door to the nice family's home and invites Dracula in.

A vampire, however, is the wrong analogy; your machine is now a zombie—the living dead controlled by some external force. A body still able to function physically, but stripped of the former person's mind and conscience. No zombie has the internal wherewithal to throw off the shackles of the zombie-master and re-exert their own willpower. Only external intervention, zombie-killers, can stop the living dead.

Technically, your computer is now a bot—in a botnet—run by a botmaster or bot-herder.

Today's programs of choice to download onto your infected machine are capable of taking full administrative control of your operating system:

- siphoning all data and communications on your computer or smartphone, and at periodic intervals—usually at least once daily—sending it back "home" to the C&C server; and

- downloading any programs the infiltrators want your machine to perform without your knowledge. This can range from setting up infected links to other (now zombie) computers, through sending spam or acting as a transit point for illegal data, to participating in a cyber-attack against a country. All of this while you are reading the latest news and checking your bank account.

A short stroll through history shows that, if you were part of one of the TDSS/TDL4 botnets, you were one of 5.5 million zombies; if you were part of the original ZeuS, you joined 3.6 million in the USA alone; and if part of Koobface, you were in the company of another 3 million. The BredoLab virus, dismantled by the Dutch authorities in 2010, contained 30 million bots; the early Mariposa botnet had nearly 13 million bots when it was taken down—some place the count above 20 million. As long ago as 2009, China's Office of the State Council issued a white paper, "The Internet in China," stating that 18 million Chinese computers were infected by the Conflicker virus on a monthly basis—around 30% of the nation's computers.

New contenders for pride of position emerge continuously to join the older workhorses. Fortinet identified ZeroAccess—a bitcoin [Internet e-currency] mining botnet—as the leading threat in the first quarter of 2013. If you inadvertently downloaded this malware, you were one of 3 million reported during this time, with 100,000 new infections swelling the ranks weekly.

Bots from busted botnets cannot necessarily be subtracted from the total number of infected machines unless there is proof the malware was removed from each individual computer and they were protected from further re-infection.

This is extremely difficult; finding and checking individual machines across continents is hard enough. But with today's self-replicating malware that works not only bot-to-botmaster but also bot-to-bot (P2P: person to person), cleaning out zombies can be close to impossible. As Rik Ferguson of Trend Micro noted: "The Mariposa framework had infected nearly 13 million machines and that framework is still alive. The fact that the guys were arrested didn't take the botnet out."[18]

Not all botnets are as large as TDSS and Mariposa. Many number bots in the hundreds, thousands or hundreds of thousands. Small specialized botnets with specific targets—from certain industries and government sites to particular kinds of data like financial and medical—have been gaining popularity over the last several years.

More things you can do with a botnet:

"A botnet can be leveraged in many different ways. Anyone can rent botnet resources, and harness the power of many individual machines on the network… For a relatively small amount of money, a single individual can level the playing field in competition with larger organizations. This is the appeal of the botnet, in the minds of many hackers globally. In the minds of most everyday network users, a botnet is nothing more than a high tech extension of common, organized crime. In the minds of anyone who is paying attention, they raise some serious security concerns."
— *Mohit Kumar*[19]

1) rent a botnet.

By the hour—for less than ten dollars; or by the day, month, or any custom period of time. Websites renting botnets can be both highly sophisticated—offering botnet services by preferred type of attack, target audience (banks, government officials, social-media, smartphones), geographic location, intended goal, etc.; and highly artistic—evoking a sense of poetic creativity in the users.[20]

An evolving trend among top-end botnet-rental services is to offer customer-support services packages—variously including tutorials, advanced hacking services, tech support, data collection and analysis, and sales outlets (including payment means) for the pilfered data.[21]

2) rent an infected computer or smartphone in a botnet as a proxy for your Internet traffic.

This allows a person to anonymize their Internet traffic. There is even a Firefox plug-in to make it easy to use the proxy system. In mid-2011, Peter Bright wrote that this rental cost about $100 a month;[22] and, as Brian Krebs' blog shows, the prices are continually falling.

3) rent space to host illegal content.

Bot-herders with fast-flux DNS configurations can rent these services to people who want safe web-space for illegal content like child pornography. Fast-flux DNS provides a means to avoid detection by pointing the domain name of the site to a different set of host IP addresses in very quick succession, sometimes as often as every one to three minutes. The hosts are often compromised computers that are then used as web servers without the victim's knowledge.

4) rent a botnet to make a botnet.

BOT-GLOBAL

> *"At the most basic level, botnets are nothing more than tools, and there are as many motives for using them as there are variants of them. The most common (and arguably most potent) use is to conduct some sort of cybercrime."*
>
> – Gragido, Molina, Pirc, Selby[23]

An estimated 53,000 botnet command and control servers are currently on the Internet.[24]

Returning to Gunter Ollman's estimate that 15% of all Internet-connected computers are bots—in real-time, this means that, of the 1.7 billion or so computers connected to the Internet, 255,000,000 are zombies.

That doesn't include the rapidly increasing numbers of smartphone botnets, some now transmitted with a simple tweet or text. The infamous ZeuS malware has been tailored for cellphones and nicknamed "ZitMo (Zeus in the Mobile), and the equally popular SpyEye malware for mobile devices has been dubbed "SpitMo." They are joined by other successful smartphone botnets running programs—like DroidDream, Android.Bmaster, AnserverBot, iKeeB, and TigerBot at the time of writing—with new, more sophisticated malware emerging regularly. While reliable statistics are hard to glean, many suggest mobile-phone infection rates are reaching those of computers.

The end is not yet in sight. Mohit Kumar discusses the next step in crime-ware in an article entitled "Who needs a botnet when you have a 4-Gbps DDoS Cannon?"[25] He explains that the DDoS (Distributed Denial of Service) world is moving from "complex small scale Botnet attacks to much larger network based attacks, perpetrated largely by hijacked web servers." The impact can be substantial. Large-scale DDoS attacks need a fire-power that, until now, required upwards of hundreds of servers across multiple hosting platforms. But now, Kumar explains, the same fire-power can be managed with a single DDoS Cannon, and potentially from a single server.

Endnotes

[1] "The Cyber-Crime Landscape," *BriefingsDirect* Interview with Joseph Menn by Dana Gardner, *http://soa.sys-con/node/2116303/print*. Accessed Feb 5, 2012.

[2] Howard Schmidt (White House Cybersecurity Coordinator), speaking at McAfee Public Sector Summit in Arlington, VA 4/11/2012 (cited in *The Hacker News*, Aug 2012:14).

[3] Gunter Ollmann, "Household Botnet Infections," CircleID Internet Infrastructure, March 26, 2012, *http://www.circleid.com/posts/print/20120326_household_botnet_infections*. Accessed June 10, 2012. See also Damballa's annual Threat Reports.

[4] Large-scale global research on botnet infestations conducted by a Dutch team headed by Professor Michel van Eeten of Delft University of Technology in 2011 that found 5 to 10 percent of all domestic computers (note this refers to computers alone) are regularly linked to criminal bot-networks. With typical humor, BBC reporting on this summed up: "More than one million households in the UK are believed to be harbouring criminals inside their family PC." Mark Ward, "Botnets: Hi-tech crime in the UK," December 5, 2011, *http://www.bbc.com/news/technology-15792257?print=true*. Accessed June 1, 2012.

[5] Ibid.

[6] Jon Thompson, "Botnets: the New Battleground of Cybercrime," *Tech Radar*, Oct 3 2010, *http://www.techradar.com/news/internet/botnets-the-new-battleground-of-cybercrime-719804?artc_pg=2*. Accessed December 10, 2011.

[7] *http://lastwatchdog.com/6-8-million-24-million-botted-pcs-internet*.

[8] SophosLabs, 2012 Threat Report.

[9] A 2011 variant of the data-stealing Duqu Trojan ushered in another disturbing trend by injecting into the running processes (avoiding disk access), and validating with a signed key recognized as a legitimate website (however rogue/stolen that key may be). *http://www.zdnet.co.uk/news/security-threats/2011/10/26/mcafee-why-duqu-is-a-big-deal-40094263*.

[10] Jonathan Broussard, Black Hat 2012 Presentation; and personal interview, Las Vegas, 7/28/2012.

[11] Yazan Boshmaf, et. al., "The Socialbot Network: When Bots Socialize for Fame and Money," *ACSAC*, 11 Dec. 5-9, 2011, Orlando, FL. ACM 978-1-4503-0672-0/11/12, 2011.

[12] *http://www.arstechnica.com/security/news/2011/07/4-million-strong-alureon-botnet-practically-indestructable.ars.*

[13] Lucian Constantin, "Kelihos cybercriminals rebuilding botnet," April 3, 2012, *http://security.networksasia.net.print/8452.* Accessed 5-18-12.

[14] John Leyden, "Microsoft botnet smackdown caused collateral damage, failed to kill target—Zombies just won't stay underground," *The Register*, 6/13/2013, *www.theregister.co.uk/2013/06/13/ms_citadel_takedown_analysis.* Accessed 8/16/2013.

[15] See: *en.wikipedia.org/wiki/Botnet.* Accessed 8/16/2013.

[16] Dan Goodin, "TV-based botnets? DoS attacks on your fridge? More plausible than you think," April 22, 2012, *arstechnica,* April, 2012, *http://www.arstechnica.com/business/2012/04/tv-based-botnets-ddos-attakcs-on-your-fridge-more-plausible-than-you-think.*

[17] Claire Elliott, "Botnets: To what extent are they a threat to information security?" *Information Security Technical Report* 15, 2010:102.

[18] Quoted in Thompson, op. cit.

[19] Mohit Kumar, "The Dynamic Evolution of the Botnet," *The Hacker News*, Aug. 2012, Issue 13 p. 5, *www.thehackernews.com.*

[20] Elliott, op. cit., 84.

[21] See Krebsonsecurity.com for excellent discussions and international examples.

[22] *http://www.arstechnica.com/security/news/2011/07/4-million-strong-alureon-botnet-practically-indestructable.ars.*

[23] Will Gragido, Daniel Molina, John Pirc and Nick Selby, *Blackhatonomics: An Inside Look at the Economics of Cybercrime*, Waltham, MA: Elsevier Press, 2013:81.

[24] Vitaly Kamluk, (chief malware expert for Kaspersky Lab's Global Research and Analysis Team), Web conference, Sept 27, 2011.

For real time visual graphics of global bot-statistics, organizations like Shadowserver, the Swiss Security site abuse.ch, and TrendMicro run such popular sites as bot, C&C, and malware global counts over time; ZeusTracker and SpyEyeTracker; and global botnet threat activity maps.

[25] Mohit Kumar, "Who needs a botnet when you have a 4-Gbps DDoS Cannon?" *The Hacker News*, 4/24/2013, *https://thehackernews.com/2013/04/who-needs-botnet-when-you-have-4-Gbps.* Accessed 8/16/2013.

Business

~ CN ~

"The computer threat is the most significant threat we face as a society. The threat is real. Everything we do is electronically transferred. It's the DNA of our companies.

"Businesses are attacked over the weekend, and out of business by Monday—I see this every single day. The integrity of data itself is at risk. You may not be able to trust your data. It's not just that someone who got into your system looked at your files—but that they added, or changed, something. I see companies that lose $10 billion of Research and Development strategy, work they've been developing for more than ten years, over a single weekend—and I see it again and again. The problem is much broader and deeper than most realize; and since 90% of what goes on is happening in the classified world, it's not seen by the general population.

"I WOULD ARGUE: YOUR DATA IS BEING HELD HOSTAGE
AND THE LIFE OF YOUR ORGANIZATION IS AT RISK. AND
WE AREN'T PREPARED: I CAN'T TELL YOU HOW MANY TIMES
THE FBI KNOCKS ON THE DOOR OF A COMPANY AND TELLS
THEM THEIR COMPANY HAS BEEN BREACHED—WE KNOW
BECAUSE WE STUMBLED ACROSS THE COMPANY'S INTERNAL
DATA OUTSIDE THE COMPANY IN ANOTHER CONTEXT—AND
THE COMPANY SAYS IT IS NOT POSSIBLE THAT THEY'VE
LOST DATA. AND WE ACTUALLY HAVE THE COMPANY'S DATA
IN HAND THAT WE GOT SOMEWHERE ELSE TO PROVE THE
THEFT TO THEM!

"THE STATUS QUO IS UNSUSTAINABLE.

"IN THE FBI WE LEARNED THE VALUE OF THE CON-
STITUTION, CIVIL LIBERTIES, AND THE BILL OF RIGHTS—
IT'S REALLY IMPORTANT TO RESPECT THEM. CIVILIANS ARE
ON THE FRONTLINE OF THE BATTLE EVERY SINGLE DAY,
AND THAT IS YOU. THE GOVERNMENT CAN'T DO IT ALL. I
IMPLORE ALL OF YOU TO BE COMMITTED, BECAUSE THE
STAKES ARE THAT HIGH. THE LINE BETWEEN GOOD AND
EVIL IS THIN, AND I IMPLORE YOU TO HOLD THAT LINE.
FAILURE TO STEP UP NOW WILL BE THE FAILURE OF OUR
SOCIETY."

– SHAWN HENRY—FORMER FBI DIRECTOR,
BLACK HAT PLENARY 2012

THE ENLIGHTENMENT'S legacy is mapping the world
in terms of physical geographies and structures. If you are asked
to visualize Lockheed Martin or MIT, chances are your mind's
eye envisions a mock-up of buildings with people coming and
going around various rooms filled with desks holding computers,
state-of-the-art "things" being built, and communication lines and
roadways linking these places to the larger world.

Such a view tends to give the impression that the "product"—a
new fighter jet from Lockheed Martin or an innovative computer

technology at MIT—is the ultimate valuable. Valuables, then, tend to be seen as "tangibles-in-places."

A new globe has evolved.

Information comprises the landscapes, 0s and 1s link into networks of meaning. Cyber-elite—whether white, gray, or black hat—can graft another dimension onto the traditional globe. For example, Lockheed Martin and MIT might well appear to security personnel and cyber-intruders as flows of data generated by internal personnel, linking to flows of data with other partner institutions as well as to the personal private-life data exchanges of employees while at work—generating a data-flow-scape whose perimeters little match the physical structures of the institution, and which sprawl across international borders along Internet connections.

Information, as virtually all digital analysts write, is the currency of the cyber-era.

In such a view, a vulnerability in a Microsoft, Linux, or Mac program anywhere along these interconnecting data-flows is as powerful an entry point to an institution's valuables as a key to the gold of Fort Knox. In other words, in the 21st century no one wants the F-35 fighter jet or the innovative computer program in and of itself—they want the code behind it all.

These realities do not define military and government industries alone; business in general runs on the control of innovation. Profit does not rest in a breakthrough drug, a new car model, a superconductor, the latest runway fashion, bio-infused nanotechnology, or a civilian-launched space module. It resides in the ideas and blueprints behind the products.[2]

In the two decades since the Internet emerged as a public global reality, the economy in general has moved from defining value primarily in physical assets to realizing intellectual capital makes up the bulk of corporate value.

The cyber underground has shifted its focus to the theft of corporate intellectual capital—the new currency of cybercrime. Intellectual capital encompasses all the value that a company derives from its intellectual property including trade secrets, marketing plans, research and development findings and even source code.[3]

The cyber-security firm McAfee cites Ocean Tomo Intellectual Capital Equity's estimates of the value of intangibles at around 81% of S&P 500 companies' value, noting that a significant portion of this "is represented by patented technology, trade secrets, proprietary data, business processes, and go-to market plans."

Secrets, McAfee writes, comprise two-thirds of the value of businesses' information portfolios.[4]

How fast the cyber-underground has shifted to stealing intellectual capital, and how quickly business "value" in general transformed from material-based to information-based can be seen in a few numbers. In one example, Rodney Joffe, a senior technologist at Neustar Inc. (an Internet infrastructure company), used Neustar's forensic logs to assess 168 of the largest 500 U.S. companies by revenue for cyber-intrusions. He found evidence that 162 of them owned computers that had been transmitting data out to cyber-intruders.[5]

Ponemon Institute's *2012 Cost of Cyber Crime Study: United States*[6] found:

- All industries fall victim to cybercrime (to different degrees).
- The companies surveyed report 102 successful attacks a week. The year before, Ponemon found an average of 72 successful attacks per week.[7]
- The annual cost per company ranges from $1.5 million to $46 million, with a median annualized cost of $8.9 million. Smaller-sized organizations suffer a much higher per capita cost than larger ones.

- The average time to resolve a cyber-attack is 24 days, with an average cost of $591,780 per organization.[8] Resolution time and costs increased 42% from the previous year's study—the latter itself showing a 67% increase from the year before.[9]

In the words of Larry Ponemon, chairman of Ponemon Institute, the technologies that cyber-criminals are using are beyond the capacities of most security systems: "We're defenseless against those attacks; it's a big problem and it's only getting worse."[10]

The costs extend well beyond monetary considerations and the confines of the companies suffering attacks. An investigation of the collateral damage of economic crime found organizations reported 28% damage to employee morale, 19% to reputation and their brand, and another 19% to business relations.[11]

Given these realities, PwC's findings from an international study of cybercrime[12] surveying 3,877 higher-level executives in 78 countries are unsettling. Thirty-four percent said they experienced economic crime in the last 12 months. One in ten who reported fraud had losses over US$5 million. However:

- 11% of the respondents didn't know if their organization had suffered any type of fraud during this time.
- More concerning, 44% of those who didn't know were Senior Executives.

Cyber-analyses tend to favor data over value judgments. But in this case, PwC added:

> While we do not expect executives at this [senior] level to know the type, significance or cost of every economic crime their organization had been a victim of, we at least expect them to know about the more serious ones....

We hope that the 11% who didn't know are not taking a "hear no evil, see no evil" approach. Ignoring the issue is really asking for trouble.

Perhaps even more ominous is a written testimonial to the U.S. government in which Richard Bejtlich, chief security officer at Mandiant, stated:

94% of victims learn of compromise via third parties; only 6% discover intrusions independently. Victim organizations do not possess the tools, processes, staff, or mindset necessary to detect and respond to advanced intruders.[13]

These studies tend to focus on external cybercriminal, malicious insider, or state-sponsored attacks. There is far less research into insider white-collar economic crime and financial/business market manipulation. Initial explorations into such high-level and often inter/national activities suggest they are equally as dangerous as more recognized forms of crime. As Richard Thieme explained in a Plenary Session at the Black Hat 2011 conference:

People on the exchange of the board didn't want security specialists to stop intrusions. It was because these Stock Board Groups were doing the intrusions to get insider info for their own trading.

Of the few who have investigated elite financial and business cyber-profiteering, some suggest the actual technological dangers—the potential to cause systemic inter/national institutional collapse—must be taken seriously.[14]

Perhaps my favorite current headline while writing this was: "Either we have figured out how to change the speed of light, or the Stock Exchange just got hacked." In the most concise explanation:

The Fed announced that it would not be tapering its bond buying program. This news was released at precisely 2 p.m. in Washington "as measured by the national atomic clock." It takes seven milliseconds for this information to get to Chicago. However, several huge orders that were based on the Fed's decision were placed on Chicago exchanges two to three milliseconds after 2 p.m. How did this happen?[15]

The problems do not stop at stealing, changing, and deleting data. One in four companies representing critical civilian infrastructure (i.e. energy, oil/gas, water sectors) say they have been victims of extortion through cyber-attacks or threatened cyber-attacks, according to a survey of 200 IT executives in 14 countries.

The authors of the research—Baker, Filipiak and Timlin—note that US intelligence officials attribute power outages in several countries to cyber-extortion. The study found that no industry is immune to cybercriminals: extortion cases are equally distributed throughout the various sectors of a country's critical infrastructure.[16]

Considering cyber-intrusion in general, Baker, Filipiak and Timlin found that 85% of the IT executives reported network infiltrations; 80% faced large-scale denial-of-service attacks (whereas the previous year, half said they never had); and two-thirds stated that they frequently (at least monthly) find malware designed for sabotage on their system.[17]

This research points out the increasingly blurred boundaries defining economic and military actions, and the dangers inherent in this. The authors write that the constant probing and assault faced by these crucial infrastructures was a startling research discovery, which led them to conclude:

> Our survey data lends support to anecdotal reporting that militaries in several countries have done reconnaissance and planning for cyberattacks on other nations' power grids, mapping the underlying network infrastructure and locating vulnerabilities for future attacks.[18]

"What we found," the authors conclude, "is they are not ready."[19]

Endnotes

[1] PwC, "Cybercrime: Protecting against the Growing Threat—Global Economic Crime Survey," November 2011, www.pwc.com/crimesurvey.

[2] Symantec found an estimated 49 percent of the worth of organizations is derived from the information they own. Survey based on the responses from 4,506 organizations/IT professionals in 36 countries. Symantec, "State of Information—Global Results, 2012," Cupertino, CA: Symantec, p. 7.

[3] McAfee/SAIC, "Underground Economies: Intellectual Capital and Sensitive Corporate Data Now the Latest Cybercrime Currency," McAfee/SAIC report, 2011(1-20):3.

[4] ibid., 6.

[5] Joseph Menn, "Hacked Companies Fight Back with Controversial Steps," *http://www.reuters.com/assets/print?aid=USBRE85G07S0120618*. Accessed June 15, 2012.

[6] Ponemon Institute, "2012 Cost of Cyber Crime Study: United States," Traverse City, MI: Ponemon Institute, August 2011.

[7] Ponemon Institute, "Second Annual Cost of Cyber Crime Study—Benchmark Study of U.S. Companies," Traverse City, MI: Ponemon Institute, August 2011. The 2011 study found Web-based attacks, denial of service, malicious code, and malicious insiders account for 90% of organization's cybercrime costs.

[8] McAfee/SAIC, op. cit., 1-20. In this 2011 study, McAfee found that organizations averaged a total cost of US$1.2 million for a data breach.

[9] Ponemon Institute, "Second Annual Cost of Cyber Crime Study," op. cit.

[10] David Goldman, "The Cyber Mafia Has Already Hacked You," July 27, 2011, *http://money.cnn.com/2011/07/27/technology/organized_cybercrime/?iid=EAL*. Accessed 9/12/2011.

[11] PwC, op. cit.

[12] ibid.

[13] *www.uscc.gov/hearings/2012hearings/written_testimonials/12_3_26/bejtlich.*

pdf. Quoted in: Will Gragido, Daniel Molina, John Pirc and Nick Selby, *Blackhatonomics: An Inside Look at the Economics of Cybercrime*, Waltham, MA: Elsevier Press, 2013:88.

[14] Scott Patterson, *Dark Pools: High-Speed Traders, A.I. Bandits, and the Threat to the Global Financial System*, New York: Crown Business, 2012.

[15] Kevin Drum, "Somebody Stole 7 Milliseconds from the Federal Reserve," *MotherJones*, September 24, 2013, *http://www.motherjones.com/kevin-drum/2013/09/somebody-stole-7-milliseconds-from-the-federal-reserve*," see also: Neil Irwin, *Washington Post*, *http://www.washingtonpower.com/blogs/workblog/wp/2013/09/24/traders-may-have-gotten-last-weeks-fed-news-7-milliseconds-early/*.

[16] Stewart Baker, Natalia Filipiak, Katrina Timlin, "In the Dark: Crucial Industries Confront Cyberattacks," McAfee/Center for Strategic and International Studies, 2011:6.

[17] See as well: Ponemon Institute, "2013 State of the Endpoint," Traverse City, MI: Ponemon Institute, December 2012.

[18] Baker, Filipiak, and Timlin, op. cit., 5.

[19] ibid., 5-7.

PIRACY

~ LC ~

MY FIRST FLIRTATION with piracy was short lived. When I was in seventh grade, a friend downloaded LimeWire, one of the earlier file-sharing programs, onto my family computer. My siblings and I all watched in awe as he demonstrated how we could now download any song we could think of! Our visions of a future free from the tyranny of iTunes died quickly. My mother heard that file-sharing was illegal, and immediately insisted that we delete LimeWire from our computer.

LimeWire may not have been on the family computer anymore, but piracy was at the front of my mind. News stories about piracy dooming the entertainment industry were featured on my Yahoo homepage daily. I was half-convinced that I would live to see the end of the music industry, that Hollywood would go bankrupt due to this widespread creative theft, and that authors would never be able to survive with free versions of their texts drifting about. Creative work as we knew it was doomed.

Time passed, however, and the promised creative apocalypse never came. In fact, the opposite seemed to be occurring. A creative revolution was indeed ushered in by the advent of the Internet, but it was not the catastrophe that had been predicted. Instead, a golden age of music, television, and software arrived.

This piracy scare happened to coincide with my own piracy phase, during which I was quite taken with pirates of the swashbuckling variety. It was inevitable, then, that I began to draw parallels between the two groups of criminals. Pirates of both sorts are criminals. This, however, is an oversimplification. To say that piracy is "bad" reduces it to its legal status, and ignores the other side effects. Piracy on the high seas, for instance, brought a level of democratization previously unseen in the Western world. Pirate crews elected their captains, and could vote him out of office if he failed to take into account their needs. Early piracy was regulated by necessity—as Captain Jack Sparrow puts it in *Pirates of the Caribbean*, the only real rule is "what a man can do, and what a man can't do." I would modify Captain Sparrow's statement slightly, and amend it to what people want to do, and what they do not want to do.

While modern piracy obviously is not the same as its namesake, I believe the two are analogous in their democratization of a process previously controlled solely by powerful companies and countries. Piracy allows individuals to enter into a trade route previously reserved for record labels and movie distributors. To take someone else's work and not compensate them for it is, of course, a crime, and I do not mean to endorse the activity. That being said, a fear of piracy and a dismissal of the crime as something completely illegal blind us to real solutions. Piracy, to my mind, is a microcosm of cybercrime in which both the serious problems and the incredible opportunities are presented by the Internet for the individual and the entertainment industry alike.

Pirates are both adversary and audience. They are stealing a product, yes, but they are also helping to advertise this. In television, this raises difficult questions. The delicate dance of legitimate television and piracy is perhaps best seen in HBO's response to piracy. *Game of Thrones*, according to TorrentFreak, is consistently the most pirated show on the web—its past two season finales breaking pirating records—and yet the show is hardly struggling. In fact, HBO spends an impressive $6 million budget *per episode*. With such an expensive show, it would make sense for HBO to try to really crack down on piracy—wouldn't it? And yet, the producers and directors of *Game of Thrones* do not seem too fussed about the piracy statistics. They have even gone so far as to say that it is "a compliment of sorts," to quote HBO programming president Michael Lombardo. HBO is on record as condemning piracy. At the end of the day, however, it makes economic sense for them not to "send out the *Game of Thrones* police."

Why? It makes economic sense for HBO to go easy on piracy. The alternatives, like making HBO GO (HBO's online option that currently comes only as part of the cable package) available for independent purchase, will mean losing valuable cable customers. Those pirates may become paying customers, but only if they are allowed to watch and get addicted to the show in the first place. If HBO is unwilling to make their content available online to non-subscribers, especially internationally, piracy is going to be inevitable. More accessible shows are pirated notably less often. Online access, whether paid or free, cuts television piracy drastically. Television and movies available on Netflix or Hulu experience significantly less piracy.

It all goes back to that basic idea: people do what they want. It seems that people want to follow the law but, even more than that, they want to watch their favorite shows when and where they want. They are searching for a legal way to enjoy these shows; however, if they can't find an easy and immediate way to get access to them, they turn to the plethora of illegal options that are always at their disposal.

Doctor Who recently broke international ratings records with its simulcast of the season premiere. Was this premiere just so much more popular than the past versions? Perhaps, but the more obvious explanation seems to be that making the show available to international audiences at the same time as its original airing cut down on the motivation for pirating the show. The same phenomenon has been seen on other shows as well. Try finding a pirated version of a Hulu show—*The Simpsons*, for instance. Because these shows are already available online, it is less likely that someone will take the time to make an illegal version easily available online. The community already seems to be self-regulating. People understand that their favorite shows do not come for free, and have responded well to crowd-funding ventures that invite them to place their own value on the show.

The music industry has undergone its own revolution. The Internet has offered artists a way to break free from the four multinational companies that control the industry. Whereas previously, only already successful artists could walk away from their labels, bands can now start up independently and sustain their own growth. They can reach audiences directly through musical downloads, even if they are losing some revenue to piracy along the way.

In 2007, Radiohead famously made its album *In Rainbows* available to fans only through digital download. Fans could purchase expensive physical copies, but had to do so online. Even more shockingly, let people choose how much they paid for the album. Predictably, the piracy rates on the album plummeted. And the result? Many people downloaded the album for free. However, more people also downloaded the album as a result of the buzz.

Thom Yorke told *Wired* magazine, "In terms of digital income, we've made more money out of this record than out of all the other Radiohead albums put together, forever—in terms of anything on the Net. And that's nuts." He went on to say that this was not meant to be a model for anything—just a solution.

As HBO and Radiohead have both demonstrated, piracy can be channeled for good. They have managed to create insane amounts of buzz around shows that would have otherwise reached a much smaller audience by allowing piracy to exist. Confident in their ability to provide a superior product to the shaky, virus-ridden torrents on the Internet, HBO allows people to upload their copyrighted material knowing that it will ultimately increase their sales. Panic! At the Disco and Fall Out Boy both rose to fame through social media, all those years ago, through an instinctive understanding that the publicity was worth giving away their work for free—at least for a while.

Now, I am in no way advocating the theft of creative work. Studios invest their own capital into a project, and they then get to decide how they distribute it and how they charge fans to view it. The sense of entitlement inherent to piracy is, of course, wrong. However, with this being said, I also think it is important for studios to consider their customers. I think that there is a void in entertainment—namely, a lack of online content and immediate availability—that the corporate world is just beginning to bridge. Through these small crimes, people have been demonstrating what they want. If they are given legal options, I firmly believe that the majority of people will follow legal channels to get the products they so love. Netflix and similar digital-distribution services, not astronomical fines against offenders, is what will really deter piracy.

Which leads us to SOPA... The Stop Online Piracy Act (SOPA) is infamous on the Internet as the sleazy attempt of Hollywood bigwigs to infringe on Internet freedoms. Perhaps even more unpopular is its younger cousin, the Cyber Intelligence Sharing and Protection Act (CISPA). Both were overturned after mass online outrage led by Internet activists and major web companies like Google and Wikipedia. When, in 2013, Congress finally reopened after a shutdown—and the near economic collapse of the United States government—CISPA was one of the first bills they attempted to revive. Their constituents were not happy. The conflict is clear: lobbyists with big money at stake want to be sure their property is protected, and voters want to know that their rights will be respected. To me, however, there does not need to be a conflict. If companies focus on working with the tide of Internet traffic rather than trying to dam the flow of popular demand, they will find that no one has to lose for the other to win. Reasonable availability is mutually beneficial.

Open-source software is another instance of a time when mutual cooperation can reap great rewards for both sides. To me, open-source software marks a triumph in the work of cooperation online. First, software prices are absolutely insane. Many, marketed primarily to corporations, can cost more than any individual can reasonably afford. Student discounts can help the struggling college student out, but what about the amateur video editor who can't make ends meet? The Final Cut Suite costs $1395.99. The Pirate Bay becomes an increasingly alluring option when something is so expensive.

Of course, the developers can make a compelling argument for why the product is priced this way, but one fact remains: it is hard to price something that, theoretically, costs nothing to give. It is one of the problems with the anti-piracy ads that state "You Wouldn't Download a Car." Well, why wouldn't you? I probably would—if I could have a car without taking anything from anyone else.

Pirates aren't stupid. They understand that intellectual property, despite lacking physical value, has worth. The monopoly so many software companies hold, however, leaves them completely free to decide exactly what that intellectual property is worth. As my dad always says, everything is worth what you can get someone to pay for it. As long as there are corporations ready to shell out thousands for software, companies have no incentive to price it lower.

Enter open-source software, which allows people to work together both on developing software and also on collaborating when it comes time to redistribute said software. Most famously, the Linux kernel was developed as open-source software, and—though it was not the first—it began a large-scale turn to open-source development. How can you pirate something that is made to be shared? Some people still find a way, but piracy rates plummet through this sort of collaboration.

I hope to eventually enter the entertainment industry. I want to work in television, and so the piracy of television is something that simultaneously fascinates and terrifies me. However, I think the fear is misplaced. Is piracy making major cuts into traditional revenue sources? Yes. But people are demonstrating again and again that they want to pay for products they love and support artists they identify with. The piracy problem is best solved through innovation, through finding new ways to make use of a changing international market, rather than legislation that does nothing but punish people who have found an alternate (albeit illegal) solution to the problem of distribution. Piracy is a problem, but it is also a solution. When we start looking at the way people are choosing to consume goods, we can find better ways to legally channel these goods to them.

Interview with Unnamed Man
Black Hat 2011
(Hallway Conversation)
~ CN ~

THERE'S ANOTHER FORM of intelligence out there. If you want to see how it looks to people outside the professional security world, treat me like a criminal in this conversation. I'll stay nameless, and I'll tell you what these new technologies—these new developments—look like to transnational organized crime groups.

Criminal groups have become more organized—for example, the Mexican drug lords who have taken over the government of Mexico. As people fight back, they take the path of least resistance. This is an important point to understand.

You can see this in the way the countries' electrical grids are organized, and even the monitoring systems of large companies—they take the path of least resistance. It's more efficient. But this doesn't produce secure systems. Look, in places like Mexico, governments and industries are finding out they can't control water and power grids. The computer systems running all these are vulnerable.

Organized crime groups get controlling malware into critical infrastructure, then contact the government or private industry, and say: "Pay us X amount of money and we won't shut down your ... [name it: power, dams and water, whatever]." Or they can shut down a grid and say they'll turn it back on when they get money. They can hold a town hostage like this.

As criminals are becoming more organized, they're moving into new frontiers. For example, they can hold banks hostage. It can get ugly—they can just release the information and not even divulge that the bank's been breached.

You can see the ramifications.

On a positive note, as people start to put more solar power in their houses, the system becomes more robust, harder to control. Diversifying provides solutions.

But going back to the dangers of criminal attacks, look at cloud technology. It seems so magically advanced. The word alone conjures up a vision of a place free of the restraints and threats of the earth-bound, a place above us—like God—safe, wise, enduring.

In truth, cloud technology is like a mainframe. You're talking one big system control. When that goes down, all of it disappears. When a criminal does this on purpose, we have two options. We can pay to get it back or fight.

If security worked today, we wouldn't have our asses handed to us on a daily basis.

The Italian mafia hasn't gone away; they've become political, legitimate. And so it goes, new criminal organizations get embedded in political systems.

What's good or bad, evil or not evil, is all based in perception. Whaling is bad today; a hundred years ago it was necessary.

Ideas are evolutionary. Our evolution—all of ours, the world's—is all tied together.

I have an idea, and six other people on the planet have it too—you can be sure of it—because developments, innovations, and evolution are based on context. Powered flight, for example, was invented in three countries in the same year, 1909, as it was in the USA.

Look at the talks here at Black Hat. Look what's already possible. And ask yourself: where else is this taking place, and to what purpose?

Medical
~ CN ~

"Hope they wont [sic] infect my respirator and kill me."

— Anonymous[1]

I HADN'T GIVEN MUCH THOUGHT to murder by computer until Marc Goodman mentioned to me in 2011 that a person could murder someone by hacking his or her pacemaker.[2] The ramifications extend well beyond what we traditionally think of as medical and legal. As Goodman, an academic and former Interpol cyber-agent, explains:

> Even if a case were to go to the coroner's office for review, how many public medical examiners would be capable of conducting a complex computer forensics investigation?
> The evidence of medical device tampering might not even be located on the body, where the coroner is accustomed to finding it, but rather might be thousands of kilometers away, across an ocean on a foreign computer server.[3]

The following month, threat intelligence analyst (and diabetic) Jerome Radcliffe hacked his own insulin pump during his talk at Black Hat 2011 to show the ease with which someone can break into digital medical devices. The "ease" was financial as well as technical: while hacking a transmitter used to require thousands of dollars of equipment, Radcliffe used an Arduino module that cost less than $20. The computer-security giant McAfee upped the ante. Barnaby Jack, then one of the company's researchers:

> demonstrated a system that could scan for and compromise insulin pumps that communicate wirelessly. With a push of a button on his laptop, he could have any pump within 300 feet dump its entire contents, without even needing to know the device identification numbers.[4]

Some take such threats "to heart:" former US Vice President Dick Cheney recently disclosed that his pacemaker's wireless feature was disabled in 2007 for fear of terrorist assassination.[5]

Security specialists began to write that hospital computing systems were becoming a top site for cyber-intrusion and data theft—joining the elite ranks of business and banking targets. In 2012, 94% of healthcare organizations surveyed admitted experiencing at least one data breach in the past two years; 45% reported more than five.[6]

In the USA, where medical costs and insurance have been beyond many people's means, buying or renting someone else's medical identity is a booming industry.

We know little to date about malicious intrusion into people's medical records—nation-wide patterns of cyber-attacks to change prescriptions, add or delete data from medical records, or gather private information. Nor is there as yet much objective information on what is actually being done with stolen medical data. This can, for example, run the gamut from being sold to less scrupulous businesses considering job applicants, to insurance companies, private investigators, prospective spouses, and to "anyone" for such things as blackmail, lawsuits, and, as Marc Goodman notes, murder and assassination.

However unpleasant these possibilities are, they all involve human intention. Now a new threat is being uncovered. A classic example is the Kaspersky Lab Security report "Software Update Site for Hospital Respirators Found Riddled with Malware." The website for a US-based hospital equipment supplier that distributes software updates for a wide range of medical equipment, including ventilators, was permeated with malware—and installing attacks on people's medical devices as they updated their running programs.

> For example, about six percent of the 347 Web pages hosted at Viasyshealthcare.com, a CareFusion Web site that is used to distribute software updates for the company's AVEA brand ventilators, were found to be infected and pushing malicious software to visitor's systems.
>   The software downloaded from Viasyshealthcare.com included 48 separate Trojan horse programs and two scripting exploits.[7]

The report goes on to note that, after being contacted by Kaspersky's Threatpost, CareFusion removed links to the infected websites for respirators, but "the company still offered links for parts and supplies for CareFusion's 3100A High Frequency Oscillatory Ventilator (HFOV) and LTV series ventilators that were likewise infected."[8]

The malware was originally discovered by Kevin Fu, a medical-device security specialist, when he was downloading an update for the AVEA ventilators. It was *not* discovered by CareFusion, their cyber-security firm, or anti-malware.[9]

Fu noted that these infections pose a major risk for hospitals using CareFusion products, and wrote that he's seen vendors download pacemaker-related software from the Internet.[10] Though he reported this case to the U.S. Federal Food and Drug Administration, he points out that the agency lacks a way to track and respond to cyber-security reports for medical devices.

The CareFusion case is being investigated by the Department

of Homeland Security, and Kaspersky reports that, to date, little is known of the source of the malware. Since attacks commonly use legitimate websites to distribute malware, it is unclear if the attackers even knew that the compromised websites hosted software for life-saving devices.

Dangerously, some manufacturers will not allow any modifications to their equipment—even with security updates. In some cases regulatory restrictions uphold these bans on improving security.[11]

> "I find this mind-boggling," Fu says. "Conventional malware is rampant in hospitals because of medical devices using unpatched operating systems. There's little recourse for hospitals when a manufacturer refuses to allow OS updates or security patches."[12]

Death by botnet.

Perhaps the most heartfelt aspect of this report was an anonymous comment posted at the end of the article that read: "Hope they wont [sic] infect my respirator and kill me."[13]

The problem of malware on medical devices extends far beyond the CareFusion example. *MIT Technology Review* reported on a Fall 2012 meeting of academic researchers and government officials on this topic. Mark Olsen, chief information security officer at Beth Israel Deaconess Medical Center in Boston, discussed how malware slowed down fetal monitors in intensive-care wards for women with high-risk pregnancies:

> It's not unusual for those devices, for reasons we don't fully understand, to become compromised to the point where they can't record and track the data. Fortunately, we have a fallback model because they are high-risk [patients]. They are in an IC unit—there's someone physically

there to watch. But if they are stepping away to another patient, there is a window of time for things to go in the wrong direction.[14]

Olson went on to say that a wide variety of devices were vulnerable, ranging from compounders (preparing intravenous drugs and nutrition) and blood-gas analyzers to nuclear-medical delivery systems and half-a-million-dollar magnetic resonance imaging [MRI] machines. This could potentially result in a device's values being changed without the software knowing, or rendering the machine unusable entirely.

The malware, Olson explains, is often associated with botnets. Once it infects a computer, the program tries to contact command and control servers. The device could then potentially come under the control of the outside bot-master, and infect other devices on the medical center's network.

Kevin Fu added that these examples are a "drop in the bucket," and that thousands of other patient-care devices that are net-connected are similarly vulnerable to malware infection.[15]

Both Olson and Fu said that these problems are widely shared among medical facilities, and that malware infections of hospital equipment are rarely reported to either state or federal regulators—making solutions difficult.

"According to Ponemon Institute's Second Annual Survey on Medical Identity Theft, *we estimate that more than 1.49 million Americans have been targeted by this crime. With an average cost per victim of $20,663 the total national economic impact of medical identity theft crimes is more than $30 billion."* [2011]

– Experian[16]

Entire states in the U.S.A. are being targeted. Utah's Department of Health (UDOH) was broached in spring 2012, when nearly a million records were stolen from a computer server storing Medicaid and Children's Health Insurance Program records. At least one out of six Utah residents was definitely affected, UDOH confirmed, and said the information stolen could include:

> sensitive personal health information from individuals and health care providers such as Social Security numbers, names, dates of birth, addresses, diagnosis codes, national provider identification numbers, provider taxpayer identification numbers, and billing codes.[17]

Utah is offering a year of credit-monitoring services to those affected, but Robert Charette notes that many of the Social Security numbers stolen are those of children—and these are highly desirable to identity thieves as they can be used for a very long time without being discovered.[18]

Utah isn't alone in being a cyber-target.[19] The U.S. Department of Health and Human Services' Office for Civil Rights reports that since 2009 (to early 2012) there have been more than 420 security breaches involving around 19 million patients and their records.[20]

Data breaches are expensive as well as dangerous: at present the average economic impact for healthcare organizations over the last two years is $2.4 million dollars. Annually, Ponemon estimates, the average cost of data breaches to the healthcare industry could be as high as 7 billion dollars.[21]

The impact to those who have had their medical records stolen is still largely uncalculated—even given the fact that 52% of healthcare organizations surveyed said they had one or more incidents of medical identity theft.[22] Studies to date have tended to focus on the impact losses have on healthcare providers, largely ignoring the risks to consumers—"a fact some experts find mind-boggling."[23] Tania Karas discusses some of the more obvious dangers:

- one or more imposters obtains medical care under the victim's identity;

- the imposter's records are then merged with the victim's own records, which can lead to grave consequences if the victim receives inappropriate treatment or medicines based on the illicit user's health data;
- the fraudulent data is notoriously difficult to purge from victims' records;
- stolen data can be used to submit false claims, and to get cash back;
- this can saddle victims with high premiums;
- victims can be held liable for the bills and, unlike credit cards, there are no industry measures to limit consumer liability in medical-record fraud.

Though Karas' list stops here, I would add, among other things: the unscrupulous can use this data to manipulate lawsuits, civil actions, employment and educational considerations, political contests, and coercion.[24]

The widespread adoption of wireless mobile devices in medicine opens new threat horizons. The vast majority of healthcare organizations in the USA now use mobile devices to collect, store and/or transmit patient information—much of it sensitive.[25] Many as well link to patient critical-care devices, from pacemakers to neonatal support systems.

Wireless mobile devices are vulnerable to hacking on many fronts, and exploits circulate widely in the public domain. Yet an astounding 69% of healthcare organizations surveyed do not secure their wireless medical devices.[26]

Jeremy Simon sums up the possibilities in his article entitled: "Hacked to Death."[27]

Endnotes

[1] Anonymous, comment 1, 06/15/2012-12:20pm in: Paul Roberts, "Software Update Site For Hospital Respirators Found Riddled with Malware," *Threatpost*, June 15, 2012, *http://threatpost.com/en_us/blogs/website-distributing-firmware-respirators-riddled-malware-061412*. Accessed 6/15/12.

[2] See Marc Goodman's website *www.futurecrimes.com*.

[3] Quoted in Tarun Wadhwa, "Yes, You Can Hack a Pacemaker (and Other Medical Devices Too)," Forbes, 12/06/2012, *http://www.forbes.com/sites/singularity/2012/12/06/yes-you-can-hack-a-pacemaker-and-other-medical-devices-too/*. Accessed 12/6/2012.

[4] ibid. Wadhwa continued: "Jack showed how he'd reverse-engineered a pacemaker and could deliver an 830-volt shock to a person's device from 50 feet away—which he likened to an 'anonymous assassination.' "

[5] CBS News' *60 Minutes, http://www.cbsnews.com/8301-18560_162-57608256/dick-cheneys-heart/?pageNum=2*. Accessed 10/21/2013.

[6] Ponemon Institute, "Third Annual Benchmark Study on Patient Privacy & Data Security," December 2012. Traverse City, MI: Ponemon Institute.

[7] Paul Roberts, "Website Distributing Firmware: Respirators Riddled with Malware," June 14, 2012, *http://threatpost.com/en_us/blogs/website-distributing-firmware-respirators-riddled-malware-061412*. Accessed 6/21/2012.

[8] ibid.

[9] Kevin Fu, "Trustworthy Medical Device Software," in *Public Health Effectiveness of the FDA 510(k) Clearance Process: Measuring Postmarket Performance and Other Select Topics: Workshop Report*, Washington, DC: IOM (Institute of Medicine), National Academies Press, July 2011; Shane S. Clark and Kevin Fu, "Recent Results in Computer Security for Medical Devices," in *International ICST Conference on Wireless Mobile Communication and Healthcare (MobiHealth), Special Session on Advances in Wireless Implanted Devices*, October 2011; Daniel B. Kramer, Matthew Baker, Benjamin Ransford, Andres Molina-Markham, Quinn Stewart, Kevin Fu, and Matthew R. Reynolds, "Security and Privacy Qualities of Medical Devices: An Analysis of FDA Postmarket Surveillance," *PLoS ONE* 7(7), July 2012.

[10] *http://blog.secure-medicine.org/2012/06/click-here-to-download-your-avea. html*. Accessed 6/21/2012.

[11] Wadhwa, op. cit.; Roberts, op. cit.

[12] David Talbot, "Computer Viruses Are 'Rampant' on Medical Devices in Hospitals," *MIT Technology Review*, October 17, 2012, *http://www.technologyreview.com/news/429616/computer-viruses-are-rampant-on-medical-devices-in-hospitals*.

[13] Anonymous, comment 1, op. cit.

[14] Talbot, op. cit.

[15] ibid.

[16] Experian, blog post by Iponemon, 4/19/2011, "A billion dollar crime that needs an urgent response," *http://www.experian.com/blogs/data-breach/2011/04/19/a-billion-dollar-crime-that-needs-an-urgent-response/*. Accessed 12/4/2011.

[17] Robert Charette, "Utah's Medical Record Data Breach: Now Nearly 1 Million Records Thought Stolen," April 11, 2012, http://spectrum.ieee.org/riskfactor/telecom/security/. Accessed 6/21/2012.

[18] ibid.

[19] During this same period, *Healthcare IT News* published "10 of the largest data breaches in 2012...so far" in June 2012. Joining Utah's Department of Health are:

- Emory Healthcare, GA (affecting more than 315,000 patients—misplaced disks);
- South Carolina Department of Health (228,000 affected—employee theft);
- Howard University Hospital, Washington, DC (34,503 affected—stolen laptop);
- St. Joseph Health System, CA (31,800 affected—incorrect security settings);
- Indiana Internal Medicine Consultants (20,000 affected—stolen laptop);
- Our Lady of the Lake Medical Center, LA (17,000 affected—stolen laptop);
- Memorial Healthcare System, FL (9,497 affected—employee crime);
- Kansas Department of Aging (7,100 affected—stolen laptop, flash drive, files);
- University of Arkansas for Medical Services (7,000 affected—employee error).

These are simple breaches for the most part: low-tech crimes of laptop theft and employee actions. Medical establishments are generally among the least IT-secured in the industry. Michelle McNickle, 6/5/2012, *http://www.healthcareit-news.com/print/47706.* Accessed 6/21/2012.

[20] Tania Karas, "A Risky Rx for Your Digital Records," June 12, 2012, *http://www.smartmoney.com/plan/health-care/a-risky-rx-for-your-digital-records-1339525543748.* Accessed 6/15/2012.

[21] Ponemon Institute, op. cit.

[22] ibid.

[23] Karas, op. cit.

[24] The problem is growing: Ponemon reported that data breaches in the healthcare industry increased 32% from 2010 to 2011 and continue to escalate, while becoming more difficult to control. Ponemon Institute, "Second Annual Benchmark Study on Patient Privacy & Data Security," December 2011, Traverse City, MI: Ponemon Institute; and "Third Annual Benchmark Study," op. cit.

[25] Jeremy Simon, "Hacked to Death: The Risks of M-commerce in Health Care" May 31, 2012, *http://www.texasenterprise.org/article/hacked-death-risks-m-commerce-health-care.* Accessed 6/15/2012.

[26] Ponemon Institute, "Third Annual Benchmark Study," op. cit.

[27] Simon, op. cit.

Banks

~ CN ~

"Without the Internet our financial systems would collapse and our commerce would slow to a crawl."

— Joel Brenner[1]

"Gold. It's all about gold.

"But not regular gold, the sort of thing you dig out of the ground. That stuff was for the last century. There's not enough of it, for one thing…And, curiously, there's also too much of it; all the certificates of gold ownership issued into the world add up to a cube twice that size. Some of those certificates don't amount to anything—and no one knows which ones. No one has independently audited Fort Knox since [the 1950s]. For all we know, it's empty, the gold smuggled out and sold, put in a vault, sold as certificates, then stolen again and put into another vault, used as the basis for more certificates.

"Not regular gold.

"*Virtual* gold."

— Cory Doctorow[2]

ON THE FRONTIER of the Wild West in the USA several centuries back, a bank that was robbed faced tough decisions. Report the crime to law enforcement and try to catch the robbers? Tell the citizenry so they can better safeguard their money and the bank? Or keep it a secret for fear the patrons will lose trust and remove their money and other robbers will see how vulnerable you are to attack?

Little has changed in the intervening years. The answer to these questions today for many banks is a "Don't Ask, Don't Tell" policy. PwC Forensic Services found 40% of nearly 4,000 respondents in 78 countries said reputational damage is their biggest fear in dealing with cybercrime.[3] Former White House "Cyber Czar" Richard Clarke writes that experts at the Black Hat 2009 conference said:

> Their experiences dealing with the FBI had convinced most of them that it was hardly worth it even to report to law enforcement when they had been attacked.[4]

If the uninformed are thinking that a few people here get hit for some savings, a few there lose some money to credit-card fraud and illicit bank transfers, then the true scope of the problem is lost. Guardian Analytics' and Ponemon Institute's 2011 Business Banking Trust Study[5] surveyed 533 Small and Medium Businesses (SMB) about business banking fraud and found that:

- 56% experienced fraud in their banking accounts in the last 12 months, and 61% of those were victimized more than once. Small, medium, and large banking institutions are equally likely to be victimized.
- Banks are reacting to these crimes after money is stolen: in 78% of the cases banks didn't catch the fraud or recover any funds.

- Both banks and their business clients are losing money: in roughly a third of the fraud, the bank managed to keep or recover the money; in another third, they provided some reimbursement to the businesses for the money lost; and the last third victimized businesses received no reimbursement.
- 43% of the businesses moved their banking elsewhere after suffering fraud. "Trust is easily broken," notes the report, and businesses are not giving banks a second chance in many cases.

The "cyber-ante" is being upped at an exponential rate. By mid-2011 the FBI was warning banks about cyber-criminals launching DDoS (Distributed Denial of Service) attacks to shut down data transfers in and out of banks while they wire-transfer money out of the bank, thus ensuring their attack can't be stopped.[6]

Reading numbers and percentages can be brain-numbing, and the eye can skim over a number like 43% without pausing. But ask yourself, if nearly half your customers are leaving your business the first time they suffer fraud (and over 50% were hit this year), would you report this?

Worse, if you are losing considerable sums of money to fraud, and if (as virtually every cyber-expert warns) cyber-attacks are getting much more sophisticated and frequent, do you have the money to improve your cyber-security systems?

Virtually every expert I've encountered says that gathering and sharing information is the only way to begin to defeat cybercrime, but this is exactly what is *not* taking place.

While a significant percentage of cybercrime comes both from insiders in an organization and criminals in the same country, governments are increasingly concerned that foreign attacks on financial institutions and critical infrastructure can constitute acts of espionage and war as well as crime.

To take the banking industry in the USA as an example, Andrea Shalal-Esa and Jim Finkle show the links and increasingly blurred boundaries between individuals and nations, business and government, and crime and war in the cyber-realm:

> The National Security Agency, a secretive arm of the U.S. military, has begun providing Wall Street banks with intelligence on foreign hackers, a sign of growing fears of financial sabotage....
>
> The Federal Bureau of Investigation has also warned banks of particular threats amid concerns that hackers could potentially exploit security vulnerabilities to wreak havoc across global markets and cause economic mayhem.
>
> While government and private sector security sources are reluctant to discuss specific lines of investigations, they paint worst-case scenarios of hackers ensconcing themselves inside a bank's network to disable trading systems for stocks, bonds and currencies, trigger flash crashes, initiate large transfers of funds or turn off all ATM machines....
>
> About eight out of ten Wall Street firms have been infiltrated by foreign-government-backed hackers, according to Tom Reilly (head of Hewlett-Packard Co's security business).
>
> Investors are already worried about how quickly markets can meltdown, as trading is almost completely electronic and reliant on hair-trigger software. The Dow Jones industrial average crashed nearly 700 points in about five minutes on May 6, 2010, an unprecedented plunge that regulators said was exacerbated by algorithmic trading, panic and vacuums of liquidity.
>
> "What you're seeing is something that can cause a global tidal wave," said the cybersecurity expert Nigam, who had worked for News Corp and Microsoft Corp.[7]

One of the unspoken casualties of these cybercrime wars appears to be optimism. A 2011 Fundtech poll found that two-thirds of banking executives do not believe that the industry will ever be able to get the cybercrime problem under control.[8]

Curiously, these bankers' perceptions exist side-by-side with the conclusions of such researchers as PwC and the Ponemon Institute that solutions are quite "do-able," and involve sharing information and resources, developing dynamic working relationships with businesses, and "waking up" to what's going on.

What is the impact of such crime on society as a whole? If percentages are mind-numbing, then figures like 56% of banks hit with average losses of $5.6 million—or stealing 100 million customer files from Sony—can be almost incomprehensible.[9] Yet this is just banking in one country; Sony is just one company. How do people begin to comprehend the entire cyber-ecosystem of crime?

Even if we just consider the figures for the financial industry, the questions are stark: How long can a country's financial systems sustain such losses before they collapse?

Endnotes

[1] Joel Brenner, *America the Vulnerable*, New York: The Penguin Press, 2011:42.

[2] Cory Doctorow, *For the Win*, New York: Tor Press, 2010.

[3] Global Economic Crime Survey 2011, *www.pwc.com/crimesurvey*.

[4] Richard A. Clarke and Robert Knake, *Cyber War*, New York: Harper-Collins, 2012:213.

[5] Guardian Analytics and Ponemon Institute, "2011 Business Banking Trust Study," *www.guardiananalytics.com*.

[6] Matt Liebowitz, "Cybercriminals Create Online Traffic Jams to Cover for Bank Heists," *http://www.securitynewsdaily.com/cybercriminals-gameover-bank-heists-1374/*. Liebowitz explains that creating a smokescreen to cover an attack isn't limited to banks: Brian Krebs (*krebsonsecurity.com*) noted that, while Sony was fighting a DDoS attack by Anonymous in May 2011, hackers were stealing information on more than 100 million customers, including credit-card data.

[7] Reuters, "Exclusive: National Security Agency helps banks battle hackers," *Reuters*, October 26, 2011, *http://www.reuters.com/article/2011/10/26/us-cyber-security-banks-idUSTRE79P5E020111026*.

[8] *https://www.infosecisland.com/blogview/15787-Majority-of-Bankers-Say-Cyber-Crime-is-Uncontrollable.html*.

[9] In the swirl of business-related facts, the true toll on the average individual can get lost. McGlasson personalized the impact of banking cyber-crime: in 2010, financial losses due to fraudulent wire transfers average US$100,000 – $200,000 per victim. Linda McGlasson, "Cybercrime, phishing, malware report," 2010:722, Linda McGlasson, *blogs.govinfosecurity.com*. Accessed January 23, 2011.

COMPUTER SCIENCE PROFESSOR INTERVIEW
LARGE AMERICAN UNIVERSITY
DECEMBER 3, 2012
~ CN ~

THE STABILITY OF THE SYSTEM, the whole system, is dependent on cyber-intrusions staying hidden.

The currency of the realm is trust. Markets depend on trust in order for people to participate. The truth of the sophistication and extent of cyber-attacks undermines the integrity of the market—and the market ceases to operate effectively, if at all.

So you have active propaganda: "The Market Is Awesome." There are vested interests to keep the information on digital crime, manipulation, espionage, war—you name it—out of the public awareness. If you talk about these problems at all, it shows the market's vulnerabilities, and this can cause people to lose trust. They can pull their money out, stop participating, and run.

The working viability of the market depends on trust. It's a fragile system, in this way. There are severe penalties for violating trust. They are swift and decisive, or they are perceived to be.

Public perception changes in a heartbeat. Their currency is trust, so you have to protect *that*. In other words, we are protecting *trust* more than protecting the actual security of the market. If currency is motive, then profit lies in trust more than in the actual market structures and commodities. People always worry that "the market is uncertain." But, hey, the market's always uncertain. It's whether you trust it or not.

Gaining security involves sharing information on the leakages that allowed someone—a company, a government, a military, a hospital or research center—to be hacked in the first place. There is a tremendous disincentive to study this.

To begin with, it's a difficult problem. Then, on top of that, there is active encouragement *not* to study this. So, people are faced with the big question: do we put off talking about, studying, and resolving these problems and wait for a big crash in the future, or do we start working on this and face a big backlash now, given the disincentive of trust?

Cyber-threats are very cross-cutting. They access a very large number and a very wide range of different industries. This extends across complex platforms. For example, bank guys may not think of leakage from Facebook when considering their own vulnerabilities. They think about: "Did I cover my ass and make a strong password because I can't make Facebook change?" And so everyone ends up saying: "It's not my problem," and "it's not my place to change others' systems."

In the big picture, then, there is a tremendous disincentive to share, despite public encouragements to do so. There are certainly people who understand these problems. Policy people are trying to get people, industries, to share.

But there are deeper issues fueling all this. Take the very notion of uncertainty. It amplifies the normal bounds of the system. It makes highs and lows bigger, and amplifies the rate of what happens. Synchronized behavior is very bad. It highly amplifies how big a system-response gets and how far it goes. In computing, you are talking about amplification that can result in reactions that go faster than any human could possibly react.

Right now, people are banking on the belief that the system is heterogeneous enough to retain balance. This is the fundamental dynamic that contributes to merchant behavior. Unfortunately, systems don't always retain their heterogeneity and stay in balance.

The (False) Security of the Everyday

~ LC ~

IT IS ALL TOO EASY to be blinded by the banal. I found it happening to me while researching this book. As Carolyn tried to explain to me the threat of the botnet and the prevalence of cyber-stalking, I found myself unfazed. Why? I knew she was right, especially after I began to do my own research. When I thought about it, I knew she was on to something. The GPS tracker on my phone, for instance, does not turn off even when I turn my wi-fi and data off—something that scared me slightly. Quickly, however, I pushed the fear aside. I had to ask myself why I was doing this. The only answer I found was that the familiarity of technology kept it from being scary. Similar to the scenario presented in many a freshman philosophy class, the fact that something had never burned me before led me to assume it could not burn me in the future. I use digital technology all the time, but I'll be the first to admit that I do not know exactly how it works. I have a vague idea, and I fill this idea in with the popular myths I pick up from everywhere around me. I don't know, but the myths tell me, and then I *think* I know. Because I know a little bit about technology, and use it every day without event, it becomes banal, familiar, nonthreatening. The more nonthreatening it seems, the less attention I pay to its dangers and the less I investigate it—thus, the less I know, which starts the cycle all over again.

How do we break this cycle? We can start by knowing what we don't know, and questioning what security means in the face of a technological world. Do we know what is and is not possible to do online? What does security mean to us? Does it mean that people can't hack your cell phone, your pacemaker, your computer, your Facebook, your email? Or does it mean having a back-up plan if they do? Perhaps it's simply knowing people can, but hoping they won't?

We depend on our technology, and yet we know it can betray us. We are aware that the lights are off, that we are living in the dark, and that we are playing with a fire that casts great shadows. Like sailors at sea, we realize that we are a small part of a much larger thing. We navigate the Internet, and use its massive might for mundane tasks—we play Farmville with the same technology that can be used to disarm nuclear facilities. We are aware that our pedestrian uses for the cyber might at our fingertips belittle the power that slumbers on the other side of the screen. We see the shadows, and we hear stories of amazing hackers in faraway lands who can tame and control the full force of cyberspace. We view them almost as wizards, as outcasts living somewhere on the fringe, learning and honing their craft in isolation. They are the other, and they are not a part of our Internet—the shiny, well-lit street of Google paving the way to a near, infinitely large village in which we all feel comfortable and safe. There are dark houses in this village, yes, but even in the alleys of these streets we feel safe.

We are not safe. Yet we have an expertise in the everyday

workings of the Internet. We know our favorite websites as well as we do our best friends, and we can navigate the lit Internet like our hometown. With the power of Google at our side, we can search through databases of vast information and shift through fact and fiction using our well-honed bs detector. Skeptical, cynical, and savvy, we know the lit Internet well. This is not insignificant. For me, up until I began working on this book, the lit Internet was all that existed. I had moments where I realized that all my Internet know-how could be summed up by one word, "Google"; but I did not have any idea how to begin thinking about what lay in the shadows I was sure existed—like viruses. I had heard of viruses. I had never understood them, and the random destruction they caused baffled me. I could see no motive for creating them—but I knew they existed. There were firewalls, too. Those were important. Phishing schemes, scams, yes—I had heard of all these. I thought, with the electronic arrogance of a "digital native," that these were only of real concern to old people who didn't understand how the Internet runs.

I, like so many my age, failed to see cybercrime as a real threat. The Internet, to me, is not some mysterious, dark place—but rather a strange, yet familiar part of the everyday. Its authority comes not from what it is (which is nothing more than a connection between computers that is easily exploited), but what it is used for. When I see reputable companies online, I trust them—not the binary code behind the website. It is easy to be sucked into this false sense of security when Google and the US Government lend their names to websites but, as attacks on both have shown, their name alone cannot prevent the almost-inevitable vulnerabilities that come hand in hand with an Internet connection.

The security we feel with the Internet comes from how it is

used, *not* from what it actually is. In everyday usage, it feels safe. It is populated by trustworthy names—people we know, corporations we recognize. In actuality, however, the Internet is nothing more or less than a giant network of computers around the world—a network that can be exploited. Realizing that the technical reality of the Internet is independent from the cultural entity that the net has become helped me begin to see the possibilities and threats more clearly. The blindness of the everyday must be overcome in order to understand cybercrime as a real and present danger.

SUD
Silence, Underestimating, Denial
~ CN ~

> "Don't mitigate your fear. Deal with Reality.
> Have courage; it's who we are and how the world
> works."
> — Richard Thieme[1]

FUD IS ONE of the core analytical tools in the arsenals of cyber-specialists: Fear. Uncertainty. Doubt.

Specialists do not stop at asking if information is correct or not. They want to know something deeper as well. What is the motivation in making this information available? What is the intended endgame? Who is providing the information and why?

Statistics on cyber-attacks may be inflated, or they may be accurate. But either way, if they are used to create fear, uncertainty, and doubt among computer users, companies, populations, or politicians to achieve a goal, they constitute FUD—and should be critiqued as such. The goals are serious ones: companies seeking to increase sales to fearful consumers; industries seeking massive government funding in the name of security; politicians trying to justify new legislation; governments hoping to influence public opinion.

While writing this book, I found I had three short chapters addressing related issues, and combined them. The chapter's titles made me laugh: Silence. Underestimating. Denial. SUD—to complement FUD.

SILENCE

"This is not the story of an ultracompetent elite taking over the world. Instead it is a story of everyone, including the most successful operators of giant cloud services, having trouble understanding what is going on."
— Jaron Lanier[2]

The silence in general society around cyber-insecurity is deafening. The F-35 stands as a common example. The state-of-the-art fighter plane has been in the news recently: the cost overruns and the internal flaws discovered in the jet are causing heated discussions in the US government over ensuring quality and cost-oversight for the F-35s. At the current cost projections, which are estimated to be in the hundreds of billions for the F-35s, they would be the Pentagon's largest weapons program. Similar discussions are taking place in Canada, Japan, Norway, and a host of other countries that are contracting with Lockheed Martin to purchase F-35s at scores of millions of dollars per jet.

The media is replete with stories about budgetary bodies arguing the costs, engineers worried about design flaws, and political groups battling fiscal irresponsibility.

But I have not seen a general media report question whether it is a good idea to make, purchase, and/or use the F-35 after the Pentagon and Department of Defense suffered cyber-intrusions that stole the jet's diagrammatics, and after Lockheed Martin reported data breaches from external hackers.

The F-35, like most weaponry today, is highly dependent on computer systems: reprogram the code and the coordinates are no longer reliable, the payload is dropped in the wrong places, the communications are tampered with. A short engine-kill command to a compromised F-35 and a $100-million plane becomes a brick.

The examples are legion. At the other end of the defense spectrum in size, complexity, and cost is the workhorse of the air: the drone. As far back as 2011 in Afghanistan the media reported that some US drones had been hacked. The same problems are of concern with any computerized aviation vehicle, manned or not: someone else can use the drone's surveillance, weaponry, and targeting against the drone's owners.

It would seem logical, then, that some discussion would be taking place among the population regarding how defense dollars are best spent in a century facing wholly new kinds of armed conflicts.

UNDERESTIMATING

"We have seen this movie before; young talented hackers being able to achieve results with enough impact that people attribute their actions to a nation state. In the end [referring to the Comodo Hack], all this power lay in the hands of a 21-year-old hacker with an ideology."

– Haroon Meer[3]

Stuxnet has been called the game-changer, the dawn of a new era, the harbinger of cyberwar.

It has also been deemed state-of-the-art for its time. To gain this level of sophisticated innovation, many analysts posited it was the outcome of nation-level research teams, money, resources, detailed knowledge of the target computer system and long-term dedicated work.

Dillon Beresford and Brian Meixell created a program similar to the Stuxnet worm in 2011. Mr. Beresford explained that he developed this software in his bedroom, in two-and-a-half months, mostly at night in his time off from work. They did this on a limited budget, and with no previous experience of the Industrial Control Systems (ICS) they were hacking into. In an interview with the *Washington Post*, Beresford explained:

> I wanted to disprove that it would take a nation-state to pull this off. I'm like, no, I'm going to do this in my living room.[4]

Beresford and Meixell alerted the Department of Homeland Security of their findings—who confirmed their work. Distressed over the security implications, DHS asked them to cancel their presentation at a May 2011 security conference, which the two men did.

Beresford warns:

> I crushed it. All average guys, your typical hacker, could very easily replicate this.[5]

There is equally sparse public discussion on the repercussions of offensive cyber-attacks. Stuxnet, for example, is the proverbial "genie let out of the bottle" that can't then be controlled.

Duqu, Flame, and Gauss malware systems—cyber-weapons more geared to attack financial and business sectors—share strong similarities with Stuxnet. Gauss may be the "first documented use of a government-grade cyber weapon, repurposed for cybercriminal deeds as a Banking Trojan" explain Gragido et. al., and they conclude:

> The possibility of this type of cyber weapon having its payload altered by a relatively skilled hacker presents a nearly incredible hazard to society at large....

The potential commercialization of such weapons, as intimated by John Dvorak, will create a rather disturbing problem for those that originally created the cyber weapons, and couldn't manage to harness their power once it was unleashed.[6]

Shortly after Stuxnet was launched against Iranian nuclear reactors, the Stuxnet code was found posted on various sites online—making the code available to anyone who could use the Internet.

From minimizing the achievements of people like Beresford on one hand and the repercussions of government actions on the other, underestimation obscures challenges to the "fact" that a nation-state's power unequivocally supersedes that of any individual.

DENIAL

"Much as they may suffer from distributed denial of service attacks, these [critical infrastructure] industries suffer even more from what might be called a 'distributed denial of attack.'
  "Denial is an unrealistic long-term strategy."
  – Baker, Filipiak, Timlin[7]

No matter how much camaraderie exists, the moment I mention I was hacked, the same immediate change comes over almost all cyber-specialists: They roll their eyes up in a disdainful and dismissive gesture and look away, sometimes punctuated with a little snort. Then, they look back at me—like a teacher to a youngster—and say: "Everyone thinks they're being hacked, but most of the time they aren't."

No one to date has responded by asking: "Hack? What do you mean; what did you see?" I'm merely dismissed. I find myself wanting to respond:

- According to Norton's 2012 Cybercrime Report, 1.5 million adults become victims of cybercrime every day;

- Damballa's researchers found botnet software on more than 35% of all computers they monitored in 2010—a third hosted two or more different botnets. Today, smartphones are rivaling computers in infection rates. And that's just botnets—some countries are experiencing near 100% malware infection rates;

- 760 companies (including government, defense, security, financial, and business) were hit in a massive cyber-attack discovered in 2011, and many did not even know they were compromised. This was just one attack among many that year.[8]

- As General Keith Alexander (USCYBERCOM commander and NSA Director) said at DefCon 2012: "We are now in a new era—they're in; now deal with it."

So how can you say that most people who think they've been hacked are wrong? Or perhaps more important: "Why *would* you say this?" The few times I have actually asked this, people just clam up—they go the proverbial Blue Screen.

More broadly, in the majority of cases, cybercrime estimates are considerably lower than the sum total of breaches reported:

After the year we had in 2011, with data breaches happening all around us almost every day...I thought we'd see reports that counted up the better part of a half-billion records stolen—in my head I can add up a solid 300 million from big public disclosures alone—and confirm 2011 as the biggest year ever for data theft.

Heck, a quick glance at the breaches reported via DataLossDB shows that the top 20 breaches (based on amount of records breached) worldwide exceed 330 million records. In just the U.S., there were 11 individual breaches of over 1 million records each. Those 11 breaches alone totaled more than the 174 million reported in the Verizon Data Breach Investigations Report (DBIR). The trusty calculator shows that those 11 breaches consisted of 175,161,416 records.[9]

=✳=

There are, of course, many forms of denial—some devastating, as in the Jewish genocide during WWII; and some rather endearing, as in thinking the Cubs are going to take the World Series.

While true ignorance takes no effort at all, psychologists tell us that denial is not easy. It takes lots of energy. Historians tell us that denial often precedes the fall of the empire—Nero-fiddling-while-Rome-burned sort of thing. Anthropologists often think it has to do with power—leaders retain pride of position by controlling information. But we also know that people like happy endings. If a problem seems insurmountable, people may just shut their eyes.

Two faculty members I spoke with at a leading university cyber-research center captured the prevailing—if contradictory—attitudes about the threat ecosystem:

> PROFESSOR 1: "Cyber-threats are no different from any other kind of security issue, and we can manage these; and besides, so what if someone hacks my computer—what are they going to get anyway?"

> PROFESSOR 2: "Basically, we're toast. But a nicer way of saying this is that pretty much all major systems basic to society are compromise-able, and we don't have the answers yet."

Who in cyber-security, I was left wondering, is denying what?

I stopped a random person in the institute's hallway (who turned out to be an agreeable cyber-security engineering graduate student) and asked if his classes tended to talk about the larger realities of the "cyber-ecosystem" and its threats. In other words: who is hacking what, how are they doing it, and what does this mean for society?

> STUDENT: "Most classes never bring up these issues; we focus on the technical. Few professors ever broach these kinds of topics."

> **CN:** "Do you all tend to talk about this outside class, among your-selves?"

The student paused for a moment, as if searching for an answer that was hard to pin down:

> **STUDENT:** "Yea-No, I mean maybe some, not so much…," he said, thinking over his experiences. "I mean, we're into the technical aspects of this—that's our work, what we care about."
>
> **CN:** "Would you rather have professors talk about these larger threat realities you'll be facing at work, or leave this out of your classes?"

His answer took me by surprise:

> I'd rather have it as it is now and not talk about the systemic threats. I have chosen to have a career in security. I have to believe I can make a difference; that when I get up and go to work, I am doing something that matters, that makes a difference—that I am producing something that works.
>
> Knowing the full extent of the threats we face in the world today doesn't help me do my job any better. But it can mess me up, make it harder for me to get up and go to work and believe in what I'm doing.
>
> I'd rather not have to know and deal with it.

Stanley Cohen, in his classic work on denial, shows that not only individuals, but also entire societies can collectively engage in "not-knowing what they know":

> One common thread runs through the many different stories of denial: people, organizations, government or whole societies are presented with information that is too disturbing, threatening or anomalous to be fully absorbed or openly acknowledged. The information is therefore somehow repressed, disavowed, pushed aside or reinterpreted. Or else the information "registers" well enough, but its implications—cognitive, emotional or moral—are evaded, neutralized or rationalized away.[10]

Why is harder to answer. Part of the answer may be found in the fact that rules are few and competition fierce in the digital domain—for it is here that people find the valuable new resources that underlie political and economic power. New-era "Robber Barons" are emerging. When the dust settles, the winners take the crown.

The danger is that, in the absence of accurate *and* accepted knowledge, humans will apply what we "know" to the unknown, no matter how poorly it may match reality. As Cohen cautions, there are always powerful, vested interests seeking to control the definitions of "what we all know."

Perhaps, then, one of the most pressing problems facing us is not merely forging technological change, but also the way we think about the world.

Endnotes

[1] Black Hat 2011 conference presentation, Las Vegas, July 2011.

[2] Jaron Lanier, "How Should We Think about Privacy?" *Scientific American,* November 2013:69.

[3] Haroon Meer, "Cyberwar, Stuxnet and People in Glass Houses," Aljazeera, June 7, 2011, *www.aljazeera.com/indepth/opinion/2011/06/20116673330569900. html.* Accessed June 19, 2012.

[4] Robert O'Harrow Jr., "Cyber search engine Shodan exposes industrial control systems to new risks," The Washington Post, June 3, 2012, *http://articles. washingtonpost.com/2012-06-03/news/35459595_1_computer-systems-desktop-computers-search engine.* Accessed 6/27/2012.

[5] The Siemens Industrial Control System Beresford hacked into is used in thousands of industrial facilities. Beresford himself went on to find more than a hundred potential targets. Others have found many more, some with flaws so serious that essentially no security existed.

In a study of major control systems, researchers at Digital Bond's Basecamp Project found six of seven devices riddled with hardware and software flaws. "It was a bloodbath," project leader Reid Wightman said of their results. *www.digitalbond.com/tools/basecamp*. Accessed 8/24/2013.

[6] Will Gragido, Daniel Molina, John Pirc and Nick Selby, *Blackhatonomics: An Inside Look at the Economics of Cybercrime*, Waltham, MA: Elsevier Press, 2013:51-52. They add: "[T]he risk to all critical infrastructures by subtle reprogramming of the payload is potentially catastrophic."

[7] Stewart Baker, Natalia Filipiak, Katrina Timlin, "In the Dark: Crucial Industries Confront Cyberattacks," McAfee and Center for Strategic and International Studies, 2011:24.

[8] David Goldman, "The Cyber Mafia Has Already Hacked You," July 27, 2011, *http://money.cnn.com/2011/07/27/technology/organized_cybercrime/?iid=EAL*. Accessed 9/4/2011. Goldman notes that Kim Peretti (PriceWaterhouse-Cooper's director in forensic services) warns: "There are probably some corporations and credit cards that haven't been hacked, but you have to assume you've been compromised."

[9] Josh Shaul, "It's Data Breach Report Season: Beware of Partial Truths," 3/30/2012, *http://www.teamshatter.com/topics/general/team-shatter-exclusive/it's-data-breach-report-season-beware-of-partial-truths/*. Accessed 4/3/2012. He continues:

> Then there were another 19 U.S.-based breaches between 100,000 and 1 million records, tacking on another 5,754,299 records, giving us 180,915,715 records breached, across only 30 U.S.-only breaches. You get the picture....
>
> Ponemon says the average data breach costs 5.5M[illion], and notes that for the first time the per-record cost of a data breach has gone down (to just under $200/record). However, there is a catch. The reports only cover the incidents they cover... [As with Verizon] Ponemon's data only covers 49 breaches (I've seen counts of over 800 for the year), and they're all small breaches with less than 100,000 records stolen. I don't know what that tells us about the costs of the mega-breach—but if a small breach of fewer than 100,000 records costs $5.5M on average, it's safe to assume that a big breach (say 20 million records) is going to cost at least a few times more money."

[10] Stanley Cohen, *States of Denial*, Cambridge: Polity Press, 2001:1.

— Part Four —

Stealing Reality

STEALING REALITY
(BEHAVIORAL PATTERNS THEFT)
~ CN ~

"MAKE NO MISTAKE, YOUR PERSONAL DATA ISN'T YOUR OWN. WHEN YOU UPDATE YOUR FACEBOOK PAGE, "LIKE" SOMETHING ON A WEBSITE, APPLY FOR A CREDIT CARD, CLICK ON AN AD, LISTEN TO AN MP3, OR COMMENT ON A YOUTUBE VIDEO, YOU ARE FEEDING A HUGE AND GROWING BEAST WITH AN INSATIABLE APPETITE FOR YOUR PERSONAL DATA, A BEAST THAT ALWAYS CRAVES MORE. VIRTUALLY EVERY PIECE OF PERSONAL INFORMATION THAT YOU PROVIDE ONLINE (AND MUCH THAT YOU PROVIDE OFFLINE) WILL END UP BEING BOUGHT AND SOLD, SEGMENTED, PACKAGED, ANALYZED, REPACKAGED, AND SOLD AGAIN....

"A CHILD BORN IN 2012 WILL LEAVE A DATA FOOT-PRINT DETAILED ENOUGH TO ASSEMBLE A DAY-BY-DAY, EVEN A MINUTE-BY-MINUTE, ACCOUNT OF HIS OR HER ENTIRE LIFE, ONLINE AND OFFLINE, FROM BIRTH UNTIL DEATH."

— MARK SULLIVAN[1]

"ANYTHING DO-ABLE HAS BEEN DONE OVER THE LAST COUPLE OF YEARS. AND THEN THERE'S A GIANT VACUUM SUCKING UP VAST AMOUNTS OF DATA."

— GENE SPAFFORD[2]

STEALING MOSAIC PATTERNS
(THE EARLY YEARS)

Mosaic theory is based on the principle that a collection of disparate points of information—each utterly without larger significance in and of themselves—when added together collectively carry information of far greater significance.[3]

In the digital era, mosaic theory has become a core concern of military and intelligence agency security. It has already made its way into law: lawsuits have already been won using mosaic theory. US government agencies have sought to classify seemingly innocuous data—keeping it from legal and public view. They argue that it can ultimately be combined with other data to create larger, more meaningful composites capable of exposing sensitive national information and endangering US security.

Mosaic theory is also a cornerstone of identity profiling and, ultimately, of "stealing reality."

STEALING REALITY

MIT's *Technology Review* published an article in 2010 predicting that a new generation of malware will steal people's private behavioral patterns. Make no mistake—this does not refer to identity theft. Behavioral-pattern theft is the next generation, and a quantum jump separates the two.[4]

Up to now (pre-behavioral-pattern theft era), those collecting information on people were largely confined to external data and basic demographics: someone's name, address, sex, age, credit cards, identity-card numbers, social-group memberships, and the like. This "identity" information has been considered highly valuable and profitable: bought and sold across a spectrum of interested players ranging from legal marketing companies through intelligence agencies to identity thieves and criminal organizations.

"Identity" is public. "Identity" is consciously constructed, enacted, and controlled by a person. It is institutionalized—that is to say, it is recognized and recorded by state institutions and social bodies. It is the external projection of a person: social security number, driver's license, passport, financial account numbers, tax records, usernames and passwords, address and employment information. To steal one's car is theft; but to steal the car's registration and pretend to be the owner is identity theft.

Identity theft tends not to involve the more subtle markers that institutions confer on people like ethnic affiliation, health status, personal habits, and socio-economic ranking prejudices. People may find their wallet stolen and the cards inside used by criminals, but they are unlikely to find their religious beliefs, gaming habits, medical conditions, or love of pizza stolen.

Behavioral patterns are more valuable—a qualitative leap in what can be known about any given person and what can be done with that knowledge. "Stealing behaviors" expands from identity theft to include recording the full spectrum of people's Internet and interactional activities, the patterns they form, and how these link among individuals. With whom people communicate and how they do this, what websites they visit and what they do there, how information travels through a person's network, ad infinitum reveal intimate patterns—not only of an individual and the constellation of people, places, and topics they know and interact with, but also across the myriad interlinking constellations of others.

> This information would allow a determined attacker to build a remarkably detailed picture of the lifestyle of any individual, a picture that would be far more useful than the basic demographic information that marketeers use today.[5]

Computer scientist Yaniv Altshuler and his colleagues at Ben Gurion University call this type of attack "stealing reality."[6]

Behavioral patterns data is so valuable, these researchers write, it is almost inevitable that malicious attackers will try to steal this information by releasing malware that records links in a network. They warn that there's no reason to think this is not already taking place.

The impact is far greater than it is with identity theft. Altshuler points out that if your credit card details, online banking passwords, and account numbers are stolen, you can easily change these, limiting the damages and stopping future exploitation.

But, if your behavioral patterns are stolen by a malicious attacker, there is almost nothing you can do. Who changes their families, friends, occupation, beliefs and interests? How do people change their core behaviors?

Worse, once released (and the point of malicious attacks is to profit from the use or sale of the data), this information is almost impossible to contain. It can change hands a potentially infinite number of times for a vast range of uses.

The article on stealing reality ends with the less-than-upbeat observation that "the prospects for avoiding this new threat look bleak."

That was 2010.

Just two years later, people were speaking of an "arms race" in the personal data economy; and security experts from companies as respected as RSA were debating publicly:

Will big data know you better than you know yourself?[7]

Unsettlingly, some companies dealing in behavioral pattern data were already answering this:

We *do* know you better than you know yourself.

A "How-To" for Stealing Behaviors

"Information scientists says [sic] they need only thirty-three "bits" of infor-mation—mundane things like your zip code or the make of your car—to identify you, and the information may have nothing to do with the legal definition of personally identifiable information."

– Joel Brenner[8]

Psychographics. Identity profiling. Federated identity. Socio-Behavioral profiling. Social intelligence. NORA (Non-Obvious Relationship Awareness). Dossiers.

These sterile words all refer to the same overall process of cre-ating a deeply detailed composite of "You" linked into a deeply detailed network of all the people, places, things, activities, and ideas "You" link with in any way—and then further linked in with similar networks expanding across the world's populations in what Facebook scientists have determined is now 4.74 Degrees of Separation (down from Stanley Milgram's famous 6 Degrees of Separation).

It's done through tracking, data mining, social media mining, public surveillance, network surveillance, buying data, and steal-ing data. In one study, the *Wall Street Journal* found that out of approximately 70 popular websites that require a login

more than a quarter of the time, the sites passed along a user's real name, email address or other personal details, such as username, to third-party companies. One major dating site passed along a person's self-reported sexual orientation and drug-use habits to advertising companies....

The [WS] Journal tested an additional 20 sites that deal with sensitive information, including sites dealing with personal relation-ships, medical information and children. Nine of these sent potentially identifying information elsewhere.[9]

Craig Willis's 2011 research showed an even greater percentage of companies sharing private personal data. The Worcester Polytechnic Institute computer-scientist found that 56% of more than 100 websites leaked people's private information in ways similar to the ones discussed in the *Wall Street Journal*'s study above.[10]

Consider a few examples of information routinely collected:

> your Internet company (and anyone else who puts cookies, trackers, malware, etc. on your devices) collects your browsing information;

> your telephone company stores all your communication data, including constant updates of your GPS locations throughout the day;

> your grocery store and pharmacy have a list of every item you bought (and if you use a customer service card or credit card this is stored with your personal information);

> your bank keeps lists of all financial transactions as well as behaviors (late payments, loan activities, etc.);

> your credit card companies have records of your every purchase, as well as your purchasing and payment behaviors;

> your library, Net-TV, and video rental sites keep lists of all your activities;

> virtually any store you patronize, online or off, keeps detailed records of your transactions, and online sites keep track of all your inquiries as well;

> your school system, job, and doctor keep records not only on your grades, occupational activities, and health but also on personal characteristics, recommendations and infractions, and behavioral evaluations;

> your "Likes" (your data is recorded if you visit a page with a "Like" button regardless of whether you click that button or not);

> your government maintains your public records;

> surveillance cameras can keep time- and place-stamped

photos of you (now searchable with facial recognition software); and

> even the companies that offer monthly toll-road passes (e.g., E-ZPass, i-Pass, and i-Zoom, etc.) keep the records of where and when you passed through a checkpoint.

Any one of these businesses can generate new high-level information on any specific individual. As Jacobs explains: "For instance, supermarkets can find out, through their loyalty cards, when their female customers have their periods." Or when they are pregnant, as with the infamous department store example several years back when the company sent coupons for pregnancy products to women they had (correctly) profiled as pregnant, causing a large backlash against the store's practices. As one outraged teenager said in a famous quote: "This is *not* how I wanted my father to find out I was pregnant." Jacobs continues: "Similarly, mobile phone companies know which of their (male) customers frequent prostitute areas.[11]

Sensitive information people trust to "ethical" companies is frequently commoditized and sold on open markets like shares of pork bellies on the exchange.

> The free dating service OKCupid sent usernames to one company; gender, age and ZIP Code to seven companies; sexual orientation to two companies; and drug-use information—do you use drugs "never," "sometimes" or "often"?—to six companies.[12]

These practices at companies such as this are at least partially recognized—with enough digging, as Valentino-Devries and Singer-Vine did for the OKCupid example above.

But between these companies—whether legal or extra-legal—stand hazy gray areas of data collection that are largely invisible. The last point in the list above on toll passes is, curiously, incomplete. And it is this incompleteness that suggests the ways surveillance expands out beyond the known to invisibly penetrate unknown corners of our lives. The 2013 DefCon 21 talk, "The Road Less Surreptitiously Traveled," detailed the speaker's discovery of un-marked electronic tag readers (for car tags like i-Pass and i-Zoom) along city streets far from toll booths. He showed videos of the simple, plain dark metal readers variously affixed to structures like light poles along downtown streets, sometimes as often as every block—each one recording all the information on an individual's toll road pass. This of course includes car owner, all registration and thus public record information, time and GPS stamps, etc.[13]

This is just a partial list—one that doesn't even begin to talk about the information available on social-media sites. Add on the apps you download and (often unwittingly) grant permission to variously access your data files, contact lists, locations, browsing activities and, in some cases, to make changes to your device itself to better control and siphon information.

> The problem today is that anyone can use these tools to track you. Gary Kovacs, CEO of Mozilla, recently demonstrated Collusion, an add-on to the company's Firefox Web browser that lets you see who those anyones are. Kovacs says a who-knows-who of 150 entities was tracking his activity after one day of Web surfing. This crowd of huck-sters and ad networks was following his nine-year-old daughter, too.[14]

The list just goes on: utility usage, auto purchase and rental, dental records, magazine subscriptions, club memberships, vaca-tions, home purchase, and lifestyle records…all are ripe for "data snatching."[15] Kovacs notes, rather poetically:

> when we go on the Internet, we are like Hansel and Gretel leaving information breadcrumbs—birthdays, financial histories, relationship statuses—"everywhere we travel through the digital woods."[16]

Now the mere fact of carrying a cell phone leaves us open to profiling, and behavioral predictions. All it takes is GPS mapping—plotted many times daily by cell-tower location "pings" with your phones. Moreover, how many of us think as we text, MMS, talk, video, surf, add people to our contacts, and live out our lives on our phones that all this is fully logged? The recent public NSA debates have cast light on how accessible these logs are to authorities; but equal public attention has not yet been given to how accessible these are to other companies, intruders, and data-snatchers.

Companies (both legal and extra-legal) aggregate and analyze all these myriad bits of data collected from virtually every aspect of people's lives. What are they looking for? The examples are legion—a few include:[17]

> changes in your financial status—indicated, for example, by keywords you use on social-media sites;

> who your friends and associates are and how they are doing financially and socially—applying the "law" that "like attracts like," that those with good credit hang out together and "deadbeats befriend deadbeats," or that having a divorced friend significantly increases the odds that you will divorce. Those with "deadbeat friends" fare worse in financial and even employment applications with institutions using such background information;

> life changes, now and in the future—starting a family, falling ill, moving, etc.—all affect a person's ability to handle jobs and finances;[18] and

> the less ethical find treasure-troves of useful information that can be put to countless advantages, from assessing job and insurance candidates through social manipulation to outright blackmail, harassment or murder.

PREDICTING "YOU" IN THE FUTURE (WITH 94% ACCURACY)

"There is something both spooky and grand about the idea that our lives are part of patterns and currents still invisible to us."
— Dennis Overbye[19]

A number of researchers are showing how much can be gleaned about people from a cell phone alone. "Phones can know," in the words of Dr. Alex Pentland, director of MIT's Human Dynamics Laboratory:

> People can get this god's-eye view of human behavior....
> Just by watching where you spend time, I can say a lot about the music you like, the car you drive, your financial risk, your risk for diabetes. If you add financial data, you get an even greater insight. We are trying to understand the molecules of behavior in this really complete way.[20]

Studying the travel routines of 100,000 mobile-phone users, researchers at Northeastern University, Boston, found that people's movements followed mathematical patterns allowing them to forecast a person's *future* whereabouts with 93.6% accuracy. This held true across ages and genders, and whether people stayed close to home or traveled widely.

Taking such research a step further, Micro Musolesi, Manilo Domenico, and Antonio Lima of the University of Birmingham (UK) developed software that can predict where a person will be, within 20 meters, *24 hours in the future*—even if people deviate dramatically from their normal patterns. This marks a breakthrough in the ability to predict "breaks in routine."[21]

Reflecting on this, Sebastian Anthony notes that, on the benign side, Google Now—knowing where you will be 24 hours from now—can offer up helpful suggestions you don't know you need yet. And on a more nefarious side, the algorithm can be the foundation for "a Precrime Police Division, a la *Minority Report*."[22]

Speaking to the more Machiavellian big picture, Dr. Johan Bollen explains:

> It is not just about observing what is happening; it is about shaping what is happening. The patterns are allowing us to learn how to better manipulate trends, opinions and mass psychology.[23]

Anonymity: A Just-So Story a la Rudyard Kipling

The most common justification given for mining personal data is that this data is anonymized—that individuals' identities are removed. This is sheer sleight-of-hand—if indeed these statements are anything more than bald-faced lies.

> Strip it away—that's called "anonymizing" it—and data aggregators can put it back almost instantly.
>
> Researchers at Stanford were able to re-identify people by their Netflix viewing habits simply by comparing the company's carefully anonymized viewer ratings with publicly posted ratings on other Web sites that rated the same movies. Essentially, they showed the emptiness of the promises that Netflix and others make that you can do, watch, or buy whatever you like anonymously on their Web sites.[24]

In practice, companies may variously: 1) keep data they collect anonymized, but link these records with ones containing identifications from databases in their company or from other companies; 2) redefine anonymized, for example to mean having random raw information and then employing companies or tools capable of identifying people from this data; 3) merge anonymized data with databases that identify personal information and merge this yet again with other companies' databases culled from different sources (social-media sites, public records, web browsing, etc.); 4) keep personal information with data and just say its anonymized. Equally dangerous, third parties can buy, use, or hack "anonymized data" and, in a few steps using available tools, figure out people's identities.[25]

WHEN "YOU" ARE MORE "ME" THAN ME

"The thing that scares me most in life is someone knowing me better than I know myself."
                              – Student in my Anthropology class, 2013

There is yet a deeper, and potentially more dangerous, aspect of "stealing reality." Bob Griffin discusses Dan Gardener's explanations of what "behavior" means in the new personal-data era, and what is at stake:

> Dan was explaining the ways in which our decision-making tends to be unconscious and therefore how difficult it is for us to really understand how we make decisions. Our behavior reveals our preferences and predicts our decisions more accurately than what we say. So as more of what we do is available on-line, analysis of the patterns in what we buy, what sites we visit and so on will give reliable and predictive insights regarding each of us. These insights derivable from the big data about us may well be more accurate predictors of our behavior than our own views of ourselves.[26]

These data-profiles, the article goes on to say, can be used effectively against us. In targeting our revealed preferences, and not what we actually say, we can be blind-sided in all kinds of ways. People in general have numerous personal blind spots. We tend to believe that what we say about ourselves is true—is "us." We may not necessarily be aware of the (many) ways what we actually do contradicts who we say we are, and believe ourselves to be.

The solutions, according to Gardener, rest with what he calls "meta-cognition": whereby people begin "turning attention back on itself" so we can recognize our blind spots.

As an anthropologist, I find it curious that an antidote for the commercialized theft of behavioral patterns and the resultant attempts to control people rests neither with legal nor technological measures, but with human self-awareness through meta-cognition.

MINING

> *"As Capital One's data contractor quipped, 'We never don't know*
> *anything about someone.'"*
>
> *– Joel Brenner*[27]

The technology does not stop at monitoring offline records and online data. BlueCava, a successful data-company, has developed a means of "fingerprinting" average computer users—a "device ID" technology. This identifies a person across *different* sites, computers and smartphones, usernames, times, and reasons for online activity. That means a person who banks using a family business name on one computer, chats online with different pseudonyms on a tablet, works under a company login on a home machine, and Facebook's under their nickname on a smartphone can be identified across all these sites and devices as the same person.

One of numerous companies offering these kinds of services, BlueCava's home page announced a range of services, one example beginning:

> In today's uber-connected world, consumers use many screens to browse, shop, and connect with your business. BlueCava provides the insight you need to understand what happens across screens—every impression, every activity, and every conversion.[28]

As of mid-2012, BlueCava's CEO David Norris said they can identify devices with 99.7% accuracy.

More startling is his claim that, at that time, the company had already identified approximately 10% of the 10 billion Internet-connected devices in the world.

Christine Dudley, a legal specialist in big-data and data-mining businesses, reminds us that players like BlueCava are in fact small in comparison to the behemoths of the industry—companies like Acxiom.[29]

Innovations from different companies are further combined by data-mining moguls. Brenner writes that Microsoft created software capable of finding, linking, tagging, and correlating all electronically available images of the same subject. With a single photograph of a person—say from their passport or a surveillance camera—you can find every other photo of that person ever posted online. Furthermore, every bit of information ever associated with any of the images can be simultaneously included. Brenner points out that this can run the gamut from biometric data (such as fingerprints) to a person's "credit history, bad jokes about them from a high school yearbook, photographs, social information from Facebook, and so on."[30]

One of the main arguments against this kind of meta-profiling is that people cannot *elect* to be private—and to keep their various social roles separate. In the physical world, people can go home from work and take dance classes, write friends complaining about company policies, use recreational drugs, and have a patch of skin cancer removed without all of these groups knowing about the others. People can maintain anonymity if they so choose.

But "fingerprinting" that identifies a person even when they choose anonymity, and then links the various discrete aspects of their life into a comprehensive overarching profile that is instantly for sale can jeopardize that person's employment, insurance, reputation, safety, finances, and friendships.[31]

Underlying all this use and abuse of our personal data, Christine Dudley explains, is the fact that data cannot be owned. Only "original work" can be copyrighted, not "facts in the world." Trade secrets can have value for business and be protected, and business patents enforced. But this does not translate to the personal realm. Consequently, she shows, few data brokers are regulated, and the regulation that does exist is both limited and weak.

The bottom line is that, for the most part, "stolen" data does not exist in terms of a person's data.

Dudley stresses that researchers, legal professionals, and security experts need to approach this situation thinking like a hacker. First, data-mining companies and data-brokers find that protecting personal data offers little benefit. Like most companies to date, they find protecting *their* business data more important than the people's data they store and trade in.

As security costs money, and that cuts into profits, the business is often better protected while the individual's data is left precariously vulnerable. Since there is no accountability except in instances like credit bureaus, the risks are minimal. Dudley sums up the "Hacker Value Equation:"

Low difficulty + Low risk
+ Moderate payoff + Clean money
= Sounds great to me![32]

CREATING PEOPLE-AS-PRODUCTS

Few people outside the information industry realize the lightning speed at which an individual's transactions are transmitted, bought and sold—that is, *if* they even realize that their surfing activities are bought and sold at all. These databases are now hyperlinked, and data on individuals is commercialized literally within milliseconds of an individual's online action (e.g., opening Expedia, friending someone on Facebook). Julia Angwin observed in 2010, before the explosion in DIY [Do It Yourself] data-mining software and sales sites:

> Information about people's moment-to-moment thoughts and actions, as revealed by their online activity, can change hands quickly. Within seconds of visiting eBay.com or Expedia.com, information detailing a Web surfer's activity there is likely to be auctioned on the data exchange run by BlueKai, the Seattle startup. Each day, BlueKai sells 50 million pieces of information like this about specific individual's

browsing habits, for as little as a tenth of a cent apiece. The auctions can happen instantly, as a website is visited.[33]

This information is not randomly dumped into a box marked with a person's name—merely one of millions of unconnected bits almost impossible to sort through or make sense of. Sophisticated profiling and personality assessment algorithms are developed and applied to this massive amount of data on any person—and on the people in their social networks. To invent a word here, all this data is "mosaic'ed" into complex multi-person profiles that are further bought and sold.

Companies involved in "stealing behavioral patterns" and "complete identities" don't advertise with these words. "Predictive Analysis" and "Inductive Analysis," Sullivan notes, are preferred at present. Either way, these practices are based on taking what at first appears to be isolated, random, and innocuous information and adding it to other information to build a powerfully meaningful composite of a person.

Several of the established legal USA-based companies brokering personal data offer information on many millions of citizens. ChoicePoint has tens of billions of records on individuals and businesses. Acxiom offers, among other products, InfoBase TeleSource to companies with toll-free numbers, so a caller's name, address, and facts like the kind of home they live in, car they drive, and clubs they belong to display on the telephone's ID box.[34] Other such companies include: Alliance Data in Texas; eXelate in Manhattan; BlueKai in Cupertino, California; RapLeaf; Intellidyn—the list goes on. The most extensive individual dossiers (outside of government and intelligence agencies), most agree, are held by Google and Facebook. These now represent vast multi-billion-dollar industries.[35]

Less than two years after the research on "stealing reality" by

Yaniv Altshuler and colleagues at Ben Gurion University, Sullivan writes that some companies already use inductive models capable of assessing up to 10,000 different variables—each with its own assigned weight based on its predictive capacity—per person.[36]

So What?

"If an observer with a suitably massive computer obtained enough personal information about someone, that observer could hypothetically predict and manipulate that person's thoughts and actions. If today's connected devices might not be up to the task, tomorrow's will be.

"Many of the components to create such a service exist already."

– Jaron Lanier[37]

"So what?" is the most common answer I receive when asking people what they think of this data-mining-to-profiling.

Much of the debate today about these kinds of data collection and sales revolves around its use in advertising. A common justification is: "Ok, so we collect data on your browsing habits, buying behaviors, and online chat entries—but isn't it good to have ads sent to you tailored to your lifestyle and the things you like?"

While arguments on both sides of the personal-profiling debate rage around the issue of how this is used by advertising companies, a host of other people and businesses are quietly amassing and capitalizing on this data in ways that powerfully affect our lives.

Examples are everywhere. These dossiers have already been used in evaluating people for home sales and loans, auto purchases, legal assistance, and personal healthcare. They have been used by insurance agencies to evaluate customers, and by schools to consider student applicants.

I have seen online reports of banks buying individuals' information to assess loan decisions; employers using this data in considering job applicants; retail stores to decide how much to charge customers; businesses to evaluate whether to give custom-ers preferential (or poor) treatment—down to if calls are routed to high-service, no-waiting customer-care centers or low-budget, basic-service congested call sites. Information like this can be pur-chased from such places as the legal data-industries discussed above to graynet and darknet market-data and profile brokers.

The behavior-pattern business doesn't stop there. It can run the gamut:

- from companies that specialize in aggregating and analyz-ing entire networks of connected individuals, and whose products have been used to manipulate social trends, or for political crackdown (as shown by examples from Arab Spring demonstrations, and the Syrian government's use of computer records to imprison/torture suspected rebel sympathizers);

- to companies (e.g., CampaignGrid, Targeted Victory, and RapLeaf) that sell behavioral profiling on millions of US citizens to both major political parties seeking to influence voter actions.

People have posted warnings that this data has been used to blackmail people, illegally deny jobs, commit robbery, stalk and kill, and threaten jurors into finding defendants guilty or innocent.

The crux of the issue is that the information, and the attendant power, does not run both ways, as Michael Fertik warns with a new twist on "the 99%":

> But increasingly, data collection is leapfrogging well beyond strict advertising and enabling insurance, medical, and other companies to benefit from analyzing your personal, highly detailed "Big Data" record without your knowledge. Based on this analysis, these compa-nies then make decisions about you—including whether you are even worth marketing to at all.

As a result, 99 percent of us live on the wrong side of a one-way mirror, in which the other 1 percent manipulates our experiences.[38]

Unfortunately, in the digital-information universe, the line between legal and illegal is profoundly hazy, and often non-existent. What few laws already exist are, for the most part, tenuous at best and largely influenced by the profiling companies in their favor at worst. What stops a legal entity from collecting personal information culled from underground websites and incorporating it into their legal personal dossier sales? At 16 cents apiece to buy between 10,000 and 16,499 dossiers, as Krebs shows, the price is affordable to almost anyone.[39]

THE POST-OPT-OUT WORLD

> *"In 2006 the United Kingdom information commissioner Richard Thomas warned that we are 'sleepwalking into a surveillance society.' He referred to the increased recording and monitoring of people's behavior, for instance via security cameras, various smart cards (for identification, loyalty, access, transport), data retention for (mobile) phone and email communication, automatic number plate recognition (ANPR), radio frequency identification (RFID), biometric verification and identification, and so forth."*
>
> *– Bart Jacobs*[40]

The matrices now in use are sufficiently developed that it no longer matters if you try to restrict your data presence. You may leave a school, job, or doctor, but your records don't. You can guard your credit card and financial data like Fort Knox but that information is on the servers of companies flung across the globe. You can cancel your Facebook account, but others continue to post about the great party at your place, or the cool new trick you found to avoid paying taxes on your moonlighting job.

Being free increasingly requires being shameless. In principle, the extensive monitoring that characterizes a surveillance society does not force you to behave in a certain way. You are, in principle, still free to make your own choices, as long as you do not care about the fact that the resulting behavior is being monitored and leads to information storage out of context. If you don't care that other people know that you watch (say) adult films, via your Pay-TV subscription or via IP-addresses stored at online servers, you quite happily and freely switch them on. But if you do feel ashamed, the (knowledge of the) fact that you are being monitored may inhibit you....

The panopticon style prisons designed by Jeremy Bentham may serve as model for society as a whole, where citizens are becoming transparent and are monitored constantly, but are never sure whether their digital traces are actually inspected or not.

There is no clear separation between passive monitoring on the one hand and active influencing and controlling on the other.[41]

In many cases, that data is so poorly guarded that "script kiddies" (novice hackers) can break in and steal a company's records. A list of the major hacks on companies in the last several years shows that many gained entry through vulnerabilities in the company's computer networks that were well known and for which simple solutions were widely available. In some cases a company's customer record security is so poor, or negligent, it is deemed criminal. As I write this, the Wyndham hotel chain is facing a lawsuit claiming the business is criminally liable for the cyber-theft of many customer files (with sensitive information) because it was so negligent about computer security.

Fighting Back

"No single observer has a complete picture of who has gathered what data about whom in our world today.

"We must rely more than we might prefer to on theory, philosophy, introspection and anecdotes. But this does not mean that we cannot think."

— Jaron Lanier[42]

Those who extol the "safety" and social benefits of data-mining and information-brokering are not without challenge. Though it seems the majority of US society in general is not yet conversant in the key issues, others see anything but positive outcomes.

Patrick Moorhead maintains we now live in a kind of "digital feudal economy":

> We live on land we don't own, and we provide the masters of the realm (Facebook, Google, etc.) with unlimited free access to our data and behavior, which they monetize for billions of dollars. We get to keep our little plots of digital land for free and are otherwise pretty much at the whim of the feudal masters.[43]

Moorhead calls data—along with its control and manipulation—the new oil: "Like crude deposits buried deep under the surface of the earth, the growing sea of personal data represents a vein glory of new opportunities for businesses to reap massive financial gains."[44] At the same time, this ushers in a new era in the way people assess their value in the digital world.

The author sees people becoming more involved in managing and profiting from their own data, protecting it from the mega-data brokers through companies offering personal data vaults; but at a cost—the potential for a global personal-data breach of as-yet unimaginable proportions.

> Once these data sets are combined, it will be increasingly difficult to put them back. The fear then is all of this co-mingled personal information might be leaked into the cloud, unrecoverable. Your entire personal history of everything will be seared into the fabric of the web forever. The only recourse would be to shut down the internet and start over.[45]

Mark Sullivan concludes that these practices surrounding the personal-data economy are hidden, and they are accepted only because people don't know about them. The solution is to lift the veil of secrecy.[46]

Bruce Schneier, security technologist and philosopher, warns that we are in many ways entering a digital feudal world.[47]

Some of us, he explains, have pledged allegiance to Google—with Gmail accounts, Android phones, Google Docs and Google Calendar. Others have pledged to Apple—with Macs, iPhones, and iCloud. Still others turn everything over to Microsoft, or Amazon and Facebook. We, the users, are becoming vassals to these vendors, our feudal lords. Just try to take your data, he suggests, from one digital lord to another.

We accept this in part because most of us can't manage, and secure, the hardware, software, and systems that make our digital lives run smoothly. Feudalism provides security.

And we welcome it partly because of convenience. We like it, Schneier points out, when we can access our email from anywhere, restore our contacts when we lose our phones, find our calendar updates appearing across all our devices, and turn our back-ups over to the Cloud.

We relinquish control for security. In the new era of digital feudalism, Schneier says, trust is our only option. We trust that our data is secure, our privacies respected, our devices protected from criminals. Trust is our only option because we have no control over our feudal lords—we don't know what security methods are in place. We can't demand that the vendors show us, nor can we audit them. And most of us can't install our own security systems.

But there are risks in feudalism, Schneier concludes. "These companies own us, so they can sell us off like serfs."[48] They can make security mistakes, act arbitrarily and capriciously, mine our data and sell it off in the pursuit of profit. "Ultimately, they will always act in their own self-interest."[49] This should not be a surprise—they are, at core, profit-making businesses.

The answer, for Schneier, is for all of us to step up and make sure real security is provided for both lords and vassals. At present, there is dangerously little regulation, law, policy, or means of enforcement for businesses operating in the cyber-world—leaving them largely without restrictions or oversight.

Schneier has long been stressing that knowledge and data are the "land," the resource of the realm, in this new era.[50]

In the Feudal Era of the Middle Ages, people's physical security was at stake. Their bodies could be bought and sold, protected or harmed, but not their inner beings.

The era of "stealing reality" ushers in the previously inconceivable fact of buying and selling, protecting or harming people's innermost behaviors, their "selves." I am left wondering if in the future cyber-slavery laws will evolve against the buying and selling of "individuals" in their most profound sense?

Endnotes

[1] Mark Sullivan, "Data Snatchers! The Booming Market for Your Online Identity," *PC World* (US) 6/26/2012, *http://news.idg.no/cw/art.cfm?id= A36FB35A-9CA1-6125-AC.* Accessed 6/28/2012.

[2] Gene Spafford, personal communication, June 2012.

[3] David Pozen, "Mosaic Theory, National Security, and the Freedom of Information Act," *The Yale Law Review*, 115:628, 2005.

[4] *Technology Review*, The Physics arXiv Blog, "New Class of Malware Will Steal Behavioral Patterns," KFC, 10/08/2010, *http://www.technologyreview. com/view/421148/new-class-of-malware-will-steal-behavioral-patterns/.* Accessed 12/02/2011.

[5] ibid.

[6] *Arxiv.org/abs/1010.* 1028:Stealing Reality. This research was part of the basis for the 2010 MIT *Technology Review* article cited above.

[7] Bob Griffin, "Will big data know you better than you know yourself?" March 7, 2012, *http://blogs.rsa.com/griffin/will-big-data-know-you-better-than-you-know-yourself*? Accessed 6/28/2012.

[8] Joel Brenner, *America the Vulnerable,* New York: The Penguin Press, 2011:23.

[9] Jennifer Valentino-Devries and Jeremy Singer-Vine, "They Know What You're Shopping For," *Wall Street Journal,* December 7, 2012, *http://online.wsj.com/news/articles/SB10001424127887324784404578143144132736214.* Accessed 12/13/2012.

[10] ibid.

[11] Bart Jacobs, "Keeping Our Surveillance Society Nontotalitarian," *Amsterdam Law Forum,* Vol. 1, No 4, 2009, *http://ojs.ubvu.vu.nl/alf/article/view/91/165.* Accessed 5/14/2012.

[12] Valentino-Devries and Singer-Vine, op. cit.

[13] Pukingmonkey, "The Road Less Surreptitiously Traveled," DefCon 21, 8/3/2013. Pukingmonkey, the speaker, works as an IT Director in healthcare informatics at this time.

[14] Antonio Regalado, "High Stakes in Internet Tracking," *Technology Review,* MIT, June 4, 2012, *http://www.technologyreview.com/news/428044/high-stakes-in-internet-tracking/.* Accessed 8/16/2012.

[15] Sullivan, op. cit.

[16] Regalado, op. cit.

[17] The Financial Brand, "Datamining Social Media Profiles for Actionable Intelligence," October 24, 2011, *http://thefinancialbrand.com/20160/analyzing-social-media-networks-for-financial-marketing/.* Accessed May 14, 2012.

[18] Ken Lin, "What Banks and Lenders Know About You From Social Media," *http:/mashable.com/2011/10/07/social-media-privacy-banks/.* Accessed May 14, 2012.

[19] Dennis Overbye, "Mystery of Big Data's Parallel Universe Brings Fear, and a Thrill," *New York Times,* June 4, 2012, *http://www.nytimes.com/2012/06/05/science/big-datas-parallel-universe-brings-fears-and-a-thrill.html?ref=technology.* Accessed June 16, 2012.

[20] Robert Lee Hotz, "The Really Smart Phone," *Wall Street Journal* online, April 22, 2011. *http://online.wsj.com/news/articles/SB10001424052748704547604576263261679848814.* Accessed 12/2/2012.

[21] Sebastian Anthony, "Precrime creeps closer to reality, with predictive smartphone location tracking," August 21, 2012, *http://www.extremetech.com/computing/134422-precrime-creeps-closer-to-reality-with-predictive-smartphone-location-tracking.* Accessed 12/8/2012.

[22] ibid.

[23] Hotz, op. cit.

[24] Brenner, op. cit.

[25] See, for example, the Def Con Conference 2013 presentation "The Dark Arts of OSINT" by Noah Schiffman and Skydog, Las Vegas, August 4, 2013.

[26] Griffin, op. cit.

[27] Brenner, op. cit., 18-19.

[28] BlueCava Home Page: *www.bluecava.com.* Accessed 8/17/2013.

[29] Christine Dudley, "Strange Interactions in Personal Data: Brokers and the CFAA," DefCon Conference, 8/4/2013.

[30] Brenner, op. cit, 165-166.

[31] Sullivan, op. cit.

[32] Dudley, op. cit.

[33] Julia Angwin, "The Web's New Gold Mine: Your Secrets," *Wall Street Journal* online, July 30, 2010, http://online.wsj.com/news/articles/SB10001424 052748703940904575395073512989404#. Accessed 2/5/12.

[34] Mark Dice, "Orwellian Data Mining," July 29, 2011, *http://www. facebook.com/notes/mark-dice/orwellian-data-mining/244128125609217.* Accessed 5/14/12.

[35] Joel Stein, "Your Data, Yourself," *Time*, March 21, 2011:40-46.

[36] Sullivan, op. cit.

[37] Jaron Lanier, "How Should We Think about Privacy?" *Scientific American*, November 2013:67.

[38] Michael Fertik, "The Rich See a Different Internet Than the Poor," *Scientific American*, February 18, 2013, *http://www.scientificamerican.com/article. cfm?id=rich-see-different-internet-than-the-poor.* Accessed 3/11/2013.

[39] Brian Krebs, "How Much Is Your Identity Worth?" October 31, 2011, *http://krebsonsecurity.com/2011/11/how-much-is-your-identity-worth.*

[40] Jacobs, op. cit.

[41] ibid.

[42] Lanier, op. cit., 65-66.

[43] Patrick Moorhead, "Why Your Personal Data Is The New Oil," November 10, 2011, *http://adage.com/article/digitalnext/personal-data-oil/230932/.* Accessed 5/14/12.

[44] ibid.

[45] ibid.

[46] Sullivan, op. cit.

[47] Bruce Schneier, "When It Comes to Security, We're Back to Feudalism," *Wired*, 11/26/2012: *http://www.wired.com/opinion/2012/11/feudal-security/.* Accessed 12/02/2012.

[48] ibid.

[49] ibid.

[50] See, for example, his recent book: Bruce Schneier, *Liars & Outliers: Enabling the Trust That Society Needs to Thrive*, Indianapolis: John Wiley & Sons, 2012; and his blog "Schneier on Security."

Cellular Service Employee Interview

January 7, 2013

- CN -

"When you use Siri and/or Dictation, the things you say will be recorded and sent to Apple in order to convert what you say into text and, for Siri, to also process your requests. Your device will also send Apple other information, such as your first name and nickname; the names, nicknames, and relationship with you (e.g., "my dad") of your address book contacts; and song names in your collection (collectively, your "User Data")... By using Siri or Dictation, you agree and consent to Apple's and its subsidiaries' and agents' transmission, collection, maintenance, processing, and use of this information, including your voice input and User Data..."

> – Apple Inc. iOS Software License
> Agreement 4.(c) Siri and Dictation[1]

The Cell-phone Store was unusually empty the day I stopped in to get some fixes on my new device, with 5 or 6 employees standing at the service desk. As they were working on solving my technical issues, I mentioned I had recently read the Siri licensing agreement for users, and was wondering if people commonly agreed to it while using their phones or tablets for things they would want to keep private. Do people tend to share the same ideas about what should be private and where transparency is ok; are these changing with the digital generations, I mused? "What do you think people might ask Siri they wouldn't want people to know?" I asked them. One of the guys said: "I heard one customer say he asked Siri where to hide a dead body, and Siri came back with all kinds of answers like 'in a cemetery' and 'in a morgue.'"

When the laughter died down, one of the men turned thoughtful and said:

Asking these kinds of questions, you got to realize you're starting to deal with sensitive stuff here. You're asking people things they don't want others to know, that they don't want to talk about, unless it's in the privacy of their own home.

This is something that goes deep. Let me ask you: What do you have with you all day long? Think about it. What is always with you; something that never leaves you, never changes.

You are talking to different friends throughout the days; there's no one person you are with all day all night all the time. You change clothes, so that's not constant. You're not in your car all the time.

The one thing you have with you all the time, the only thing that is with you all day every day, is your cell phone.

You have an intimate relationship with your cell phone. It carries your good times and your bad times. Tucked away in it are the great texts and the awful ones—they tell all about the loves and heartbreaks and escapades you don't want anyone to know about.

Your phone carries your moments of genius, and the low-down

rotten things you do that you don't want to share with anyone. People have voice mails from someone who has passed, the only words they have left of someone they loved. Vacation pictures; family fights; those bad relationships; stuff you want to hide. Your phone is full of your hopes, your dreams, your failures and triumphs...and you don't let people into such a private, sometimes sacred—but always personal—place.

People's phones carry their life—they carry more than any other one person knows about them.

People don't like to let you inside their intimate relationships. These are things so personal people don't even tell their spouses. No one wants you to know the deep dirty secret they keep within themselves.

Your cell phone is a digital extension of yourself. It's like a matrix, but without the fighting. People put everything in their cell phone. They think, "Man, I don't want anyone to know this stuff"—but it's there in your cell phone.

Most of the employees had gathered around while he was speaking, and were nodding their heads in agreement—we were all swept up in his eloquence. I asked if I could quote him, and pondered: "What you say is so true, and at the same time people give this all over to Apple or whatever company they license with, and to any undisclosed 'third parties' the companies choose."

"Yeah...," he said.

Endnote

[1] Apple Inc. iOS Software License Agreement 4.(c) Siri and Dictation, *ssl. apple.com/legal/sla/docs/ios51/pdf.* Accessed January 28, 2014.

Privacy

~ LC ~

WHILE WE WERE DISCUSSING this book, Carolyn told me about Jeremy Bentham's panopticon—a circular prison designed so that guards at the center of the building could monitor all the actions of prisoners.

The Internet is a social panopticon. When you meet me, within seconds, you can place me. This is something that can be dangerous—it's hard to start over, to have a fresh slate. It's also redefining ideas of privacy.

A lot of attention is given to privacy from the government and corporations who would like to use information on you for whatever reason. This is a huge issue, to be sure, and it deserves the attention it's given. Ralph Nader's observation that "people are stunned to hear that one company has data files on 185 million Americans" rings especially true when you consider Google's new privacy policies and the latest technology in targeted ads. The government seems an equally likely culprit for exploiting the new data-mining technologies. There is a controversial scene in *The Dark Knight* where all the civilian phones are used to help find the Joker. While unfortunately it is unlikely that we are going to get a Batman anytime soon, it is certainly conceivable for the government to have the ability to collect snippets of conversation or video from your cell phone. It becomes, just as it is in the film, an issue of privacy versus security. This starts to be a hard balance to strike. On the one hand, maybe it's an invasion of privacy; but, on the other hand, it may save lives. It's a fallacious train of thought, but I can't help worrying about the slippery slope that small invasions of privacy set us on. What sort of precedent does it set if civilians' phones can be tapped—not because they are thought to be guilty of something, but because they may be in proximity to someone who might be guilty? In the movie, Batman smashes the technology so it can never be used again, but what's to assure this happening in real life? In fact, since this was originally written, it has been revealed that the NSA has been monitoring the private information of Americans online.

Whether it is the government or Google that is keeping tabs on us, the Orwellian implications of civilian surveillance are certainly scary. However, in the shadow of this monolithic threat of "the man" watching us lurks what I think may be the more deadly privacy issue. The issue of social privacy might be a lot smaller in scope and sound less terrifyingly dystopian, but I think the implications for the individual are much more real.

On September 25, 1975, Oliver Sipple saved President Gerald Ford's life when he tackled a would-be assassin in a crowd. He was heralded as a hero, but begged the press to not discuss his private life. The decorated Vietnam veteran was widely known to be gay, but he had not told his family or employer and did not want them to find out. Despite this, a columnist at the *San Francisco Chronicle* outed Sipple. The hero was fired from his job and became estranged from his family. He filed a 15-million-dollar privacy suit against the presses that published stories about his sexuality, but the court ruled that he had become a public person when he saved the president and was thus a newsworthy story, of which his sexuality was a part.

Sipple ended up ultimately committing suicide in the aftermath of the article, ruined by his accidental celebrity status.

In 1975, the newspapers were the social panopticon. If something was in the papers, most everyone knew it. It permeated the social world. The journalists who catalyzed Sipple's suicide showed a shameful lack of discretion. Now, however, the journalists are thirteen-year-olds with Twitters. Now, someone could send a tweet to the effect of "at the mall with my gay best friend" and accidently out someone. Very private information can be thrown around very quickly and very publicly. This has expanded from newspapers edited carefully by professionals to become a network of individuals sharing their own lives and the lives of those around them online.

I'm not a celebrity. I'm just a person, but the line between private and public people is beginning to be blurred. Perhaps a friend decides to use our picture for something online, and it goes viral. We're famous now, although we never meant to be, we are—and this changes the rules on what is and is not allowed.

Our online reputations permeate everything and leak into the physical world. There are even websites like Klout that try to monitor your influence online. I want to be a writer, and one of the tips I hear all the time is to have a blog, get a Twitter, get your name out there. It's constant marketing. I just read a book where people's names had monetary value, and I think that's beginning to be the case. I think, to an extent, this has always been the case. The concept of a reputation predates the digital. Now, though, it's happening on a much larger scale. We're all becoming mini-celebrities.

It's also much easier to slander. You don't know if people are being reasonable or truthful when they post things—that post about so-and-so being a slut could just as easily be the delusions of an ex-boyfriend. It isn't new; it's just a lot more visible. Your reputation follows you even if you go somewhere where no one knows any of the people you know. You can piece together a person's life story. Privacy is becoming a little bit of an illusion.

Gossip is as old as language itself, but new technology allows it to spread farther and faster and to be better archived than ever before. The line between "private person" and "celebrity" can be but a viral video away, with people inadvertently becoming famous for better or worse. Within social circles, information is quickly and publicly circulated. Within these circles, infamy can be merely one bad post away. For the individual, this can be scary. Personal attacks aren't famous, but they can spread through a friend group very quickly; and they can be archived, which means they can be dug up later. I've had friends post questionable things on my Facebook wall, and I've had to delete those posts. My great-aunt is on Facebook—I can't have posts filled with f-bombs on the top of the page!

Online, you are always in front of a crowd, and this is just going to increase. The kids of my generation will have their parents online—we're not going to get offline any time soon. We've all done things we don't want our parents to see, but is the Internet going to allow this?

One example of the all-seeing eye of the Internet is Facebook Timeline. Before, you would have to be pretty dedicated to get to posts from my middle-school years. You would have to click through years of more recent posts to go back to the day I joined Facebook. Now, however, all it takes is a few casual scrolls to find me in the midst of my awkward era. I don't have the time or the energy to hide all the embarrassing parts of my past from the public eye, but I do not like that you can instantly force me back into my sixteen-year-old skin. I said a lot of dumb stuff that sounded cool to me at the time—but I don't want prospective employers or future friends judging my ill-advised political statuses, or my misuse of the word "legit." I've changed and I've grown, but I remain constantly and publicly linked to my past. I think this is true for many people my age. Our childhood, for better or worse, is public information.

This becomes especially problematic in the context of future employers. I was always relatively careful of what I allowed to be posted online, having heard the horror stories; but a part of me always thought that my posts would be buried beneath years of other things. My freshman year of high school was not spent wondering if I'd appear ignorant to employers—I assumed they would never read through what I had written back then. If I could have imagined that Timeline would come out, I may have avoided some of the LOLs and OMGs that dominated my early status updates.

One of the issues with the high visibility built into the digital age is rumor. It's bad enough that people can see everything you've ever said or done without things you've *never* said or done also being reported as fact. First is the problem that it can be difficult, if not impossible, to distinguish fact from fiction or rumor from reality online. Second is the fact that news—whether true or false—can spread like wildfire through cyberspace. To an extent, this has always been the case. There's that old saying that a lie gets halfway around the world before the truth can get its shoes on. This is especially true in the digital age.

Another bad situation occurs, obviously, with stalking. It's something that oddly we don't talk about much. The more I think about it, the more I think it is weird that we don't talk about it. It would be so easy to stalk someone. If you got access to my phone, for instance, it's with me all the time. If you get my GPS turned on, you'd know exactly where I am. If you could read my texts, you'd know exactly where I am going to be.

Privacy and property overlap online, creating the issue of whether or not you own your own image. This concept of "property of person" can become crucial online. You may make a joke out of a picture of a friend, just to have it blow up into a meme that circles the world. One example of this is Blake Boston, who became known as "Scumbag Steve" when a meme featuring a picture of him wearing a plaid hat sideways went viral. Luckily for him, he learned to embrace his infamy and laugh about it. In an effort to be supportive of another who was experiencing this type of fame, he wrote letter to "Annoying Facebook Girl" (whose picture was used for a similar meme), in which he advised her on how to deal with her "memehood":

> You're going to be in shock for a while, when you see what people have written. But the most important and self-preserving thing you can do is know that it's not you. You can't take this personally. I'll say that again, you can't take this personally. Hell if I did...well let's not go there.
>
> The part that will suck though is that there will always be those people that somehow think YOU did this, that you made the meme, and that you could stop it if you wanted to. That you have some control over it. You don't. The internet birthed you and they'll decide when you (the meme) will die.
>
> There will also be those people who assuage their guilt by telling you how great it is, how lucky you are to be a meme. Just smile. What they are really saying is, thank god it wasn't me.
>
> So search Annoying Facebook Girl on Google images, pull up a chair with a group of your friends and laugh your fucking ass off. Cuz you know who you are and how strong you are and that, that picture has nothing to do with what makes you, you... Hopefully you'll get to where I am, feeling like some memes are hysterical. But that takes time. I'm here if you need me. I'm sorry you're hurting.

Not everyone, however, is in the position to laugh about the jokes made at their expense around the world. "I can count to potato" is a quote from *The Ringer* that made it onto the Internet as a joke about being mentally handicapped. It eventually was turned into a meme that featured a picture of a real person with real Down syndrome. The victim, 16-year-old British teenager Heidi Crowter, has tried to get the images removed, but to no avail. Facebook and the police alike have been trying to remove all the images, but they keep cropping back up.

These are very extreme instances, but they happen on a smaller scale to people everywhere. Many of my friends wake up the morning after a night out and instantly run to the computer to make sure that nothing too embarrassing was uploaded, lest their own friends see it. Everyone is very careful not to make a misstep online, because no one wants to be the social spectacle.

I guess the way I would describe it is that the Internet has a very harsh learning curve. It used to be that you'd do something dumb, and people who loved you would correct you. Now, you are corrected by people who do not even know you and clearly have no vested emotion in you. In fact, they may or may not hate you from a very limited amount of evidence—for instance, if you confuse "your" and "you're." One example of this—actually a very old, outdated example of this—is the Jessi Slaughter incident. There's a video—in fact, I'm sure there's more than one video, but I've seen only the one—in which Jessi, an eleven-year-old girl with a webcam, tries to act like she's a big deal. She says a lot of outlandish, dumb things, and it's frankly pretty offensive. Before the Internet, Jessi Slaughter would be doing her posturing among other eleven-year-olds, who may or may not have confronted her about it. Now, you've got adults basically bullying children. And it's not that she wasn't wrong—it's that she wasn't *that* wrong. No eleven-year-old deserves to have thousands of people who have never met her acting like they hate her. The video that really got to me was a video of Jessi breaking down, with her father yelling that he was going to call the cyber-police. It scared me, because something about it registered as something that could happen to anyone. But there are no cyber-police, no one to call in when it all gets to be too much.

It's a really harsh learning curve. On the internet, I've noticed myself being very afraid of making a mistake. You want to be right, and you want to have your facts straight because, if you make a mistake, it's going to be remembered. Everything on the Internet leaves traces. It can all be found and brought up. Everything you post can and will be used against you.

Does privacy even exist anymore? Everything has the potential to go public in the digital age. Texts, emails, photos, and web history can all be found and shared. Even written correspondences can be scanned and uploaded to the net by an angry third party. The potential for blackmail is enormous. Future employers may see this, people caution constantly. I know people who have been suspended from school for things they have posted online. One second-grade girl at my cousin's school had to transfer after a parent showed the principal a picture of her flipping the camera off at a sleepover. A group of girls in my high school got in trouble because they posted complaints about a teacher on Facebook, and the administration found out. There were rumors going around at my school, never confirmed, that the administration created fake Facebook accounts so they could "friend" students. Perhaps that's just paranoia, but somehow they always seemed to know exactly what was going on online. Teachers could see what was on our screens, even when we weren't at school, through a program called DyKnow (mentioned earlier) and would occasionally share this information with the entire class. We were constantly being watched, constantly being monitored. I thought this ended with graduation, but now I am beginning to realize that everyone can be monitored nowadays. The grid has become virtually inescapable.

Initially, the implications are frightening, and for good reason. It sounds like an Orwellian dystopia, with Big Brother breathing down our necks constantly. In reality, the government is not the only one watching. Stalkers have moved online to monitor their prey, and corporations collect data on people to develop target ads and profiles. Sites like Spokeo make personal information—such as one's salary, home address, phone number, age, and marital status—public and easily accessible. And all this is only what is legal and immediately visible after a quick Google search. On the Darknet, even more extensive databases exist. People could sell medical information to companies. Do companies want to have to provide expensive healthcare to a diabetic? What if you don't get that job—not because of anything you did, but simply because they know about a medical condition you have? There is also the issue of bad information, incomplete information, or malicious misinformation. What if a rumor about you gets reported as fact, and suddenly you are fired from your job for something you never did? What if a bank decides you are not a good investment based on your search history, which makes you seem like a radical Communist because of the book report you were writing on Karl Marx? The information found online is imperfect and incomplete, and thus the conclusions derived from it can be, and very often are, unreliable. Somewhere out there, a profile of you exists, and you will never be able to verify its accuracy or protest the claims it makes about you. Blackmail is no small issue in this post-private world, either. Who among us cannot be blackmailed? If we cannot be blackmailed directly, how hard would it be to find dirt on our friends and family, and control us through that?

Beyond this dismal dystopia, however, I think that the elimination of privacy could bring an unrivaled level of transparency to the world. As General Petraeus proved when his affair was discovered, not even the director of the CIA can get away with anything nowadays. If the information is accurate and readily available, perhaps the post-private world will be a better and more honest place.

BLACKMAIL?

~ CN ~

"ONE DISHEARTENING ASPECT OF THE PERIODIC LEAKS
RELATED TO THE NSA IS THAT EVEN SECRET RULES AND
REGULATIONS EMBRACED BY THE ORGANIZATION SEEMED
TO BE FUTILE. NSA EMPLOYEES USED THEIR PERCHES TO
SPY ON ROMANTIC INTERESTS, FOR INSTANCE."

— JARON LANIER[1]

THE MOST COMMON RESPONSES I hear when people
consider the impact of web and cellular tracking—of monitoring
their personal and private information—are: "So what's the big
deal?" or "What interest could people have in me?" or "What do I
have to hide?"

On the other hand, one of the more common conversations I
hear, both as an anthropologist and as a friend in daily life, is about
people worried that their families, spouses, jobs, schools, government, police, lawyers, IRS, ad infinitum will find out about their
youthful indiscretions, infidelities, cheating, stealing, drug use,
medical or emotional conditions, tax evasion, sexual predilections,
gambling habits, legal or financial problems, ad infinitum.

The two don't seem to add up to me. I know remarkably few people who are comfortable with opening up the full spectrum of their lives to public viewing, and remarkably few who are concerned that the full spectrum of their lives is being wantonly "vacuumed up" and commercialized by big business, legal and otherwise.

Equally confounding, almost everyone I know is painfully aware that there are people out there willing to buy and use the personal information of others against them: from divorce investigations and lawsuits to sports qualifications and business competition.

Yet the vast majority of public discussion on web tracking and the collection of personal data is about its use for "advertising purposes."

In exploring this seeming contradiction, it seemed to me that the easiest thing was just to ask people the question:

"What percentage of people in general can be blackmailed— if someone had access to *all* their personal information?"

Virtually everyone I spoke with said the same thing: 100%.

No one missed a beat in answering. No one pondered on the rights and wrongs of blackmail. The answers were straightforward: "100%. Everyone has something they don't want others to know."

This answer came from young people, psychologists, rich and poor, athletes, geeks, different religious affiliations, cynics and optimists. The only time I received a lower answer was among people in their 90s at assisted-living homes—people who grew up for the most part leaving their homes and lives unlocked. Their answer: 75% – 90%.

I began to expand on different examples. Most people I talked to considered what would happen if blackmailers threatened to tell the target's families, employers, communities, or law. "What

if someone on a jury was blackmailed to give a certain verdict?"
I asked. "To steal documents from work, or to leave doors to restricted areas unlocked? To throw a sports game, or harm someone?" The answers remained consistent: "Pretty much anyone can
be blackmailed."

I found one place where people felt that at least some would
stand up against blackmail. It was a tiny town, high in the Rocky
Mountains, off any major roads, on a rugged plateau with few trees,
water sources, or amenities, and an overabundance of harsh winds
and winters. The town had one main street, four blocks long, and
boasted maybe several hundred people. Ranches in the area looked
like renditions of the 1800s. Locals wore t-shirts when I visited in
August, while I was huddled in two sweatshirts.

> I don't know, gee…it'd be a hard one. But we don't much like people
> telling us what to do up here. I expect there'd be those of us who'd get
> some friends or get some guns or some information or something and
> go find the blackmailers and kinda blackmail 'em back. You know, tell
> 'em to lay off if they valued whatever it is they value.
>
> Oh sure, there'd be some who'd maybe feel like they had to give
> it up to the blackmailer—people are pretty much people anywhere—
> they got things they don't want people to know… someone gets into
> some affair, gets caught up in some business problems, their kids on
> drugs or something.
>
> But I still don't know, I mean, everyone's got problems of some
> kind or another, we all do. So what's the big deal if people find
> out—they got their own troubles too.
>
> Blackmail's just kinda against our grain up here—we don't like
> blackmailers or government or much of anyone forcing us to do some-
> thing we don't think's right. We kinda like to take responsibility for
> our own lives up here.

I finally asked Lisa the blackmail question before telling her about
the others' responses. "Oh, I don't know," she answered, "maybe

30% could be blackmailed." I raised my eyebrows in surprise. "Well," she said, "I suppose that's for serious blackmail. If you think about things like at school—people can find out something about someone and try to get them to do certain things—then maybe 75%."

I told her I was batting a pretty consistent "100% can be blackmailed" response rate. The only people besides those in the tiny Rocky Mountain community who estimated less were a group of seniors over 90 years old in an assisted-living home who figured about 75%. Thinking about it, she finally decided: "If you consider threatening a person with something about a loved one, something that could harm them, then I'd raise it to 100%."

Endnote

[1] Jaron Lanier, "How Should We Think about Privacy?" *Scientific American*, November 2013:71.

STEALING REALITY, GEN. 2
BRAIN AND DNA HACKING
~ CN ~

"THE MODERN WORLD HAS BECOME A TAPESTRY OF THOUGHT...

"MY COMPUTER (DESKTOP, LAPTOP, HANDHELD DEVICE, ANY PROGRAMMABLE INTERFACE AT MY DISPOSAL) BECOMES AN INTEGRAL PART OF MY MIND. WHAT IS EVEN MORE PROFOUND IS THAT I NOW HAVE ACCESS TO SO MANY OTHER HUMAN MINDS, INPUT FROM ALL OVER THE WORLD. SINCE AN INCREASING PERCENTAGE OF THE INPUT AND OUTPUT THAT GUIDES MY REASONING ABOUT THE WORLD AROUND ME COMES FROM MY CONNECTION THROUGH A SOFTWARE INTERFACE, WHEN THAT SYSTEM IS ATTACKED, SO AM I. MY WHOLE THOUGHT PROCESS, EVERYTHING GOING IN AND COMING OUT HAS BECOME INFECTED BY ROGUE INPUT.

"WHEN I LOOK AT IT FROM THIS POINT OF VIEW, I THINK OF MALWARE AS BEING MUCH MORE THAN JUST AN INCONVENIENCE. JUST AS A CONTAGION IN THE BIOLOGICAL ECOSYSTEM THAT KEEPS MY BODY ALIVE COULD BE AN EMINENT THREAT TO MY SURVIVAL, A MALWARE INFECTION MIGHT BE A SIMILAR THREAT TO THE CONGRUENCE OF MY THOUGHTS AND IDEAS. WHILE MY IDEAS MAY NOT BE THE ONES TO CHANGE THE

WORLD, WHAT IF THE NEXT ALBERT EINSTEIN SOLVES
AN INCREDIBLY COMPLEX PROBLEM, ELSEWHERE ON THE
NETWORK, AND AS HE REACHES CRITICAL MASS ON THIS
BREAKTHROUGH, HIS SYSTEM CRASHES AND HE LOSES THE
BRIDGE OF THOUGHT THAT LED TO HIS DISCOVERY.

"WHAT IF MOTHER TERESA LOSES FAITH IN
HUMANITY, BECAUSE SHE FINDS HERSELF UNDER WHAT
SHE PERCEIVES AS A PERSONAL ATTACK, AS SHE TRIES TO
FORMULATE A PLAN TO HELP FEED THE POOR. EMOTIONAL
HEALTH IS JUST AS IMPORTANT TO THE WORLD AS
PHYSICAL HEALTH, AND INTENTIONAL ATTACKS ON THE
PROCESS OF THOUGHT CAN BE JUST AS DESTRUCTIVE AS
AN ATTACKING, PHYSICAL ARMY. IT IS SO DESTRUCTIVE
BECAUSE THE INCARNATION OF LIFE THAT WE PERCEIVE
AS HUMAN BEINGS IS INTERNAL, WE SEE AND FEEL
EVERYTHING FROM THE MIND'S EYE."

— JOHN SHINABERRY[1]

AT THE 2012 USENIX Security Conference, six researchers gave a paper entitled "On the Feasibility of Side-Channel Attacks with Brain-Computer Interfaces."[2]

This probably flew under most people's radar—the title alone making the average person's eyes glaze over.

Geeta Dayal translates this to laypeople's terms in a *Wired* magazine's Threat-Level article entitled: "Researchers Hack Brainwaves to Reveal PINs, Other Personal Data."[3]

The researchers worked with users wearing the popular consumer-grade EEG headsets available to the general public for gaming, online interactivity, and the like. They hacked the headsets, then asked the people wearing them questions, but told them not to respond out loud. The only thing the researchers monitored was the user's brainwave data. From this data alone, they were able to deduce areas where people lived, their months of birth, where people banked, their PINs, and other personal information. The accuracy for the correct answer on the first guess ranged from 20% to 60%.[4]

Breaking into the headsets wasn't difficult. Headset companies like Emotiv and NeuroSky have "app stores" where users can download third-party applications. The apps to access EEG devices use a common API (application programming interface), and this API provides unrestricted access to the raw EEG signal. The researchers discovered that the applications have complete control over the stimuli the users receive.

They leave it to the reader's imagination to consider what stimuli intruders might introduce into brain/computer interfaces. The simplicity of their experiments, they write, suggests that more sophisticated attacks are possible. The threats are expanding exponentially as the quality of EEG brainwave-computer devices rapidly improves.

Dayal sums up their point in the vernacular:

> The researchers envision a scenario in which a potential malicious attacker could write "brain spyware" to harvest private information from the user, which could be legitimately downloaded as an app.[5]

Several years ago I listened to a talk by Bill Gates. He concluded his presentation by saying that if he were 17 years old today and working on digital innovations in his garage, he would be hacking DNA. DNA is, after all, a code sequence. Gates was talking in part about the lure of new frontiers, hacking the boundaries and the barriers of what is deemed possible. But I wonder if he was not also issuing a wake-up call.

A whole movement of people hacking biology "in their garages" exists. Mike Loukides writes that synthetic biology and biohacking today are where the computer industry was in the late 1970s—still nascent, but about to explode. The explosion in both cases is fueled by DIY (Do It Yourself) innovations moving beyond the professional confines of academia and research laboratories into hacker spaces, grassroots bio/hacking communities, amateur and artistic exploration, and entrepreneurial activity. Loukides notes that

> DNA is similar to machine language (except it's in base four, rather than binary), and in principle hacking DNA isn't much different from hacking machine code.[6]

For Loukides, the explosion in biohacking will produce innovative solutions to the world's pressing problems—from medical to environmental. Perhaps someone will identify bacteria that can ingest cellulose and produce biofuel, or that can live in a diabetic's intestines and produce insulin. Equally, it will explore the frontiers of creativity and art: as with Christian Bok's insertion of poetry into the DNA of a microbe.[7]

Loukides' piece is preceded by an unsigned note, ostensibly from the *Synbiowatch* editor, which concludes:

> Somehow he misses the point that the difference between hacking computers and hacking microbes is the difference between making a toaster and making a baby—and that the very fact that we have no idea what the results will be determines the need for oversight, regulation, and clear ethical and safety standards.[8]

Chloe Diggins and Clint Arizmendi take this a step further, saying that "hacking the human brain is the next domain of warfare."[9] The most powerful tools in this war are the brain-computer interface (BCI) technologies, and hacking these.[10] They write that, while cyberspace has been designated the "fifth domain" of war (the first four being the classical land, sea, air, and space), the human brain is emerging as the "sixth domain" of warfare.

Marc Goodman, academic and former cyber-analyst with Interpol, has long shown the vulnerabilities in cyber-systems that will lead to the proliferation of attacks into energy "smart grids," and into increasing Internet-connected home technologies (controlling home security, electricity, temperature, communications, even kitchen and heating appliances).[11]

Goodman joined Andrew Hessel and Steven Kotler to publish an article in the *Atlantic* on "Hacking the President's DNA."[12] They predict that the creation and use of personalized bioweapons against specific individuals that leave no trace is closer to a reality than many would suspect. Already, they note, the US government is covertly collecting samples of world leaders' DNA, and quote Ronald Kessler in saying that Navy stewards sanitize anything the President has touched—bedsheets, glasses, etc.—to guard his DNA. The authors say that, while to date there has been no reported use of a sophisticated bio-weapon targeting specific DNA, most of the enabling technologies to create this possibility are already in place.

Endnotes

[1] John Shinaberry, "Support Your Local InfoSec Professional," *The Hacker News*, August 2012, Issue 13:31. *www.thehackernews.com*. Accessed 9/6/2012.

[2] Ivan Martinovic, Doug Davies, Mario Frank, Daniele Perito, Tomas Ros, Dawn Song, "On the Feasibility of Side-Channel Attacks with Brain-Computer Interfaces," *https://www.usenix.org/system/files/conference/usenixsecurity12/sec12-final56.pdf*. Accessed 8/31/2012.

[3] Geeta Dayal, "Researchers Hack Brainwaves to Reveal PINs, Other Personal Data," *Wired*, August 29, 2012, *http://www.wired.com/threatlevel/2012/08/brain-wave-hacking/*. Accessed 8/31/2012.

[4] ibid.

[5] ibid.

[6] Mike Loukides, "Biohacking: The next great wave of innovation," *SynBio-Watch*, October 11, 2012, *http://www.synbiowatch.org/2012/10/biohacking-the-next-great-wave-of-innovation/*. Accessed 11/3/2012.

[7] ibid.

[8] ibid.

[9] Chloe Diggins and Clint Arizmendi, "Hacking the Human Brain: The Next Domain of Warfare," *rsn*, December 13, 2012, *http://readersupportednews.org/opinion2/266-32/15003-hacking-the-human-brain-the-next-domain-of-warfare*. Accessed 12/13/2012.

[10] ibid. Examples they give of current BCI research include the Human Connectome Project on neural data, hardening the brain against rubber hose cryptanalysis, connecting the brain to bionic limbs and robotic systems, and hacking these interfaces.

[11] See his website: *futurecrimes.com*.

[12] Andrew Hessel, Marc Goodman, and Steven Kotler, "Hacking the President's DNA," *Atlantic Magazine*, November 2012, *http://www.theatlantic.com/magazine/archive/2012/11/hacking-the-presidents-dna/309147/*. Accessed 12/8/2012.

THE (END OF) SOVEREIGN SELF
OR: PWNING THE SELF
~ CN ~

"THE MODERN IDEA OF THE INDIVIDUAL, FOR INSTANCE
SINCE KANT, IS THAT PEOPLE ARE SIMPLY AUTONOMOUS
AND FREE, WITHIN REASONABLE BOUNDS, TO TAKE
THEIR OWN DECISIONS. MODERN DEMOCRATIC SOCIETIES
ARE BUILT ON THIS VIEW....THE SITUATION IS NOT
SO SIMPLE...INDIVIDUAL AUTONOMY IS FRAGILE AND
VULNERABLE."
— BART JACOBS[1]

"WHATEVER ANYONE THINKS ABOUT THE LAW, IT IS THE
SOFTWARE THAT DETERMINES WHAT ACTUALLY HAPPENS."
— JARON LANIER[2]

THE SOVEREIGN SELF.

Western-Enlightenment views posit a sovereign-like self, and a straightforward equation of:

1 body = 1 self = 1 soul = sovereign control.

This concept is a fundamental building block of modernity. It is a truism basic to science and society today, not a question that can be interrogated. It grounds state law, social interactions, and institutional practices.

This is taken-for-granted, assumed as reality: a person *is* a self. "Self" is not something a person can try on or take off, buy and sell, or give away. Self is unique, and unique to a specific person. Modernity has no concept of an individual meeting another person with the same self, waking up to find one's very self has been stolen, or finding that it spills out beyond the confines of one's body to define two or myriad bodies as oneself.

Today, law and literature alike accept that a person *is*—as well as has—sovereign control of self. While others, from dictators to advertisers, can try to force or influence one's actions and self-definitions, no one has the self-knowledge of another. An inalienable sovereignty is thus granted to a human being, and to being human.

At the same time, modernity recognizes that people do not fully know themselves. Unconscious behaviors, subconscious beliefs, contradictory morals, hidden phobias, unexamined desires, foibles, physical expressions, emotional reactions, patterns of thought, perceptual habits, delusions and misunderstandings, irrational likes and dislikes, inexplicable transcendental experiences—all these define humans as much as they consciously define themselves. While others may be able to decode some of a person's unconscious behaviors, no one can decode them all. The observers have their own limitations and blind spots.

These are self-evident truths modernity lives by—until now.

"Identity-shift is well under way. When the context of our lives changes, all of the contents are jumbled, including who we think we are and meta-national structures. We can't help thinking inside paradigms that emerged

from prior technologies but we also can't help acting as new paradigms demand. The end of secrecy and the end of privacy are two sides of the same coin. Hackers appoint themselves as a Fifth Estate, while security and intelligence professionals tell themselves a story that filters out as much reality as it allows in. But reality won't go away, and protocols, policies, and legalities lag behind."

– Richard Thieme[3]

What happens when these ideals are encroached upon? Not by religious authorities taking responsibility for the spiritual self, nor by advertising executives crafting ideals of beauty and wealth as self-worth, nor even by socio-political leaders molding selves into self-nationals. But by unknown others claiming "ownership" [pwnage] and "use" of your "self."

What happens when meta-mosaic analysis of literally millions of data-points on any given person produces a composite under-standing that, as a Canadian Tire executive said in early 2010 (when commercial data-mining behavioral-pattern analytics were in their infancy):

> If you show us what you buy, we can tell you who you are, maybe even better than you know yourself.[4]

The tire company had already figured out, for example, that the people who buy carbon-monoxide detectors, birdseed, and pads to put on the bottom of chair legs rarely miss their credit card payments.[5]

Or, as Dan Gardener warned: "These insights derivable from big data about us may well be more accurate predictors of our behavior than our own views of ourselves." While much of the decision-making process underlying people's behaviors is unconscious, and thus opaque to them, he explains, it is transparent to the brokers of social analytics in the age of digital mega-data.[6]

Your "self," in this context, extends and circulates in critical ways beyond the bounds, and the traditional controls, of physical and conceptual personhood.

WHO LEGALLY OWNS "SELF"—HUMANS' INTERIOR INTELLECTUAL AND BEHAVIORAL PATTERNS?

> *"Future cybercrime will steal your Social Capital."*
> *– Willi Schroll*[7]

The stark question arises: who legally owns one's behaviors? This is not a question that societies have needed to ask in any serious and tangible way until now. While the knee-jerk logical reaction may be: "That's a stupid question, obviously a person owns their own behavior patterns"—one might pause a moment to consider what's actually taking place at present.[8] Willi Schroll's 2010 prediction has already come to pass: cybercrime *is* stealing your Social Capital.

Western legal systems are grounded in principles of self-sovereignty. A person has public designators and possessions that can be stolen, and this is illegal. In this worldview, it is impossible to contemplate the possibility of taking a person's internal private records and possessions—their personalities, memories, character traits, and dreams. Therefore, no laws are needed to protect against this.

Behavioral-pattern theft turns this equation on its head. What legal recourse does a person have in the face of behavioral-pattern theft, of stealing *them*? In discussing behavioral-pattern attacks as "stealing reality," Altshuler, Aharony, and Pentland explain:

> In the event of a security breach, users can also change their passwords, usernames, and credit card numbers; easily replace their email and other online accounts; and quickly warn their contacts. However, it is much harder to change one's social network, person-to-person relationships, friendships, or family ties. If a chronic health condition is uncovered through such an attack, there is no going back. Victims

of a behavioral-pattern theft cannot change their behaviors and life patterns. This type of information, once out, would be difficult to contain.[9]

Little in formal law exists to address theft of behavioral patterns and social capital.

The impact extends well beyond the legal. What does this do to self-conception in the most profound sense when a person discovers, for instance, that an unknown entity is determining whether they will or will not pay off a loan, submit to blackmail, or fight injustice; that an outsider understands the intricacies of their social networks in ways they themselves are unable to comprehend; that a complete stranger "knows"—whether accurately or inaccurately—what triggers their bad habits or creative flows when they have never been able to figure it out; or that someone else can accurately predict where they will be in 24 hours when they themselves have not yet made plans?

And what does it do to a person to discover that the "digital self" circulating of "them" may be taken by others as a more accurate portrayal than the flesh-and-blood version? That the digital self, right or wrong, can be given more weight in the world as "us"—and little possibility exists to correct this?

In this light, what are the implications of Altshuler, Aharony, and Pentland calling behavioral-pattern attacks "stealing reality?"[10] Modernity casts people as authors of their own history, their own fate—in essence, of their own reality. What are the outcomes when such "reality" is commercialized, and released beyond the confines of self-control?

Ultimately, the sovereignty of self comes under question. But what, then, replaces this centuries-old view of personhood?

Endnotes

[1] Bart Jacobs, "Keeping Our Surveillance Society Nontotalitarian," *Amsterdam Law Forum*, Vol. 1, No. 4, 2009, *http://ojs.ubvu.vu.nl/alf/article/view/91/165*. Accessed 5/14/2012.

[2] Jaron Lanier, "How Should We Think about Privacy?" *Scientific American*, November 2013:71.

[3] Richard Thieme, "Living in a Glass House when Everyone Has Stones" (Posted by Mr. Kennedy), *ITManageCast*, February 16, 2012, *http://itmanagecast.blogspot.com/2012/02/richard-thieme-in-glass-house-when.html*. Accessed 7/14/2012.

[4] Kevin Spak, "Your Credit Card Is Spying on You," *Newser*.com, April 7, 2010, *http://www.newser.com/story/85372/your-credit-card-is-spying-on-you.html*. Accessed 5/14/2012.

[5] Mark Sullivan, "Data Snatchers! The Booming Market for Your Online Identity," *PC World* (US) 6/26/2012, *http://news.idg.no/cw/art.cfm?id=A36FB35A-9CA1-6125-AC 87C18E040B4065*. Accessed 6/28/2012.

[6] Bob Griffin, "Will big data know you better than you know yourself?" March 7, 2012, *https://blogs.rsa.com/will-big-data-know-you-better-than-you-know-yourself/*. Accessed 6/28/2012.

[7] Willi Schroll, "Future cybercrime will steal your Social Capital," *future facts blog*, October 25, 2010, *http://blog.futurefacts.net/2010/10/25/future-cybercrime-will-steal-your-social-capital/*. Accessed 12/2/11.

[8] See: Christine Dudley, "Strange Interactions: CFAA and Big Data," DefCon Conference, 8/4/2013.

[9] Yaniv Altshuler, Nadav Aharony, Alex Pentland, "Stealing Reality: When Criminals Become Data Scientists (or Vice Versa)," *IEEE Intelligent Systems*, November/December 2011, p 24, *www.computer.org/intelligent*.

[10] ibid. See also: *Technology Review*, The Physics arXiv Blog, "New Class of Malware Will Steal Behavioral Patterns," KFC 10/08/2010, *http://www.technologyreview.com/view/421148/new-class-of-malware-will-steal-behavioral-patterns/*; see also: arXiv.org/abs/1010.1028: Stealing Reality. Accessed 12/02/2011.

Big Data and the Self
~ LC ~

UNDERSTANDING AND ACCEPTING the implications of big data was difficult for me. As Carolyn shared what she had been discovering, I felt myself shrink away. It couldn't be true. I was sure it wasn't true. "They can know more about you than you do," she said. She explained how banks would look at seemingly random things—such as people who had recently purchased birdseed and furniture guards—to create a portrait of that person's personality, a predictive model that attempted to see the future. In the case of the birdseed, certain purchases marked people as more reliable, thus making them better investments for a loan. Other purchases could mark one as unstable and unreliable. She explained mosaic theory, and the way information could be linked into networks so that seemingly insignificant information could become greater than the sum of its parts. Through this form of big data, she said they could create psychological profiles that could predict behaviors.

I resisted this idea. There is no algorithm that can predict behavior on the individual level, I replied heatedly. They can create big pictures and predict how masses will move with shocking accuracy, but the individuals within these systems remain enigmatic and unpredictable. I cited Durkheim, who observed that one can predict the number of suicides in Paris but not who it will be that will commit suicide, and the great paradox of complex adaptive systems—the system on the whole moves predictably even as the individual parts remain unpredictable. There is no amount of information that can tell you every inch of a person, I said, no matter how you network the information together.

Carolyn remained calm. "I never said you could know every inch of a person," she replied. I looked back over the chapter I had just read. She was right. Nowhere in her information on big data was the claim that big data and algorithms could completely and accurately predict human behavior, let alone that they could completely map the individual mind.

Why, then, had I felt so threatened by big data? When hearing about big data, my emotional response had projected an argument onto the page—as soon as I heard that a stranger could know you better than you know yourself, better than your best friend could know you, I reacted. That's not true, my gut told me. It's not right. It hit on something at my very core, because I believe, and I *need* to believe, that humans are more than just a chain of reactions that can be studied and predicted perfectly. If we are predictable, that leaves no room for true choice, for free will, for morality—we are nothing more than sophisticated robots running through pre-programmed code. The idea that algorithms and collected material can map us out suggests that we are predestined to do certain things—a notion that leaves no room for the individual mind to truly exist. It means that we do not own our own selfhood, and that our identity is merely the result of the conditions in which we were placed and the genes that we inherited. I do not believe this, but I realized that Carolyn was making none of these claims. She was simply explaining what corporations are trying to do with big data, which is to map people out with the most accuracy possible in order to better predict future behaviors and purchases.

My reaction suggests one of the threats big data holds—the information will most likely be imperfect, because there is no model that can perfectly predict human behavior. Someone who bought birdseed and was a stable investor may one day become depressed, moody, and unreliable—the bank can't take that into account with a simple algorithm. Employers attempting to evaluate workers by examining their social networks will never be able to get the full picture of the person. If they could, perhaps big data would not be so bad. If completely accurate and reliable portraits of every person in the world were created, perhaps it would be a utopia—a world of complete transparency and fairness, where everyone is correctly evaluated and valued. However, I think only a hopeless optimist would believe this to be the case. Big data ignores individual variation. All of a sudden, you are being denied a job because you bought eight cases of beer in one night as a last-minute Christmas gift for your neighbors and the company found that information from one of the many sites that sell full profiles of spending history and concluded you are an alcoholic, simply because most people who buy eight cases of beer on a Tuesday night are alcoholics. You may never even know why it happened.

Lately, privacy has been making headlines as companies like Facebook and Instagram change their privacy policies. Underneath this discussion lurks the main issue of big data—who owns your identity? I am not a particularly private person, and I don't think my life is all that interesting to strangers; therefore, I've never worried about the privacy policies of various social networks. So what if they want to keep track of who my friends are, I think as I click "agree" on another "terms and conditions" that I haven't read. Yet, by collecting all these tiny shards of the self that we share everyday online, these companies are able to put together a picture of us and claim that it is the *true* us. And they can sell this version of us—to advertisers and employers, for a start.

Talking about it makes me feel somewhat like a paranoid schizophrenic. Do I think I'm constantly being watched? Am I going to start wearing a tin-foil hat so they can't read my thoughts? Probably not—and yet, it really isn't all that crazy. There are indications that this type of profiling is happening not only on the legal level, but also on the illegal level as well. In a world where corporations are able to track and predict your behavior, who are you to say who you are? The problem with big data is not its predictive abilities, but rather its limitations. The data will be imperfect, and we will end up with an artificial and incorrect explanation and understanding of self—which then becomes a practical problem when this definition of self informs employers, banks, hospitals, and any other business or individual willing to pay for this type of information.

— PART FIVE —

WALKING INTO THE FUTURE

Transparency

~ CN / LC ~

"Relentless transparency is a fact of life."

"We are in a postprivacy, and also a postsecrecy, world."

— Joel Brenner[1]

"The experts in this field, the people who worked on information security in the Pentagon and the CIA, have known for a long time that the day would come when all of our digitized secrets would spill out somewhere....

"When that happens, we'll be left standing face-to-face with the reality of how our state functions. Do we want to do that?"

— Matt Taibbi[2]

WHILE IN THE MIDST OF WRITING, the two of us realized that, at some point, we would have to come up with a conclusion—some kind of "where is this all headed and what should we do about it?"

This hinted at a need for some kind of "solution"—for no one, least of all us, would want to end with the assessment "we're toast."

But realizing the need for a conclusion was about all we did. We left "the conclusion" a vague notion, hanging out somewhere in space. After all, we had been reading some of the greatest minds among the cyber-literati—and solutions still proved elusive.

One summer day when we hadn't talked in quite a while, we met up at a coffee shop. "So, where's it all going?" we mused, looking out over bustling city streets.

Perhaps most surprising to us was that we had independently come to the same conclusion:

- Privacy is dead.

But it isn't "just dead"—it's "more than dead." For at present we all live in cultures and with sovereign laws that still take privacy not only to exist, but to be a right. This world still accepts that, in principle and in fact, a person's inner world and private life are theirs and theirs alone to create, control, and express.

Those creating new empires built on controlling people by controlling the data that defines them—the robber barons of the digital world—have done so by killing privacy in practice while supporting it in theory. The very ideals and laws protecting privacy through the ages have become the means, the weapons, bludgeoning privacy to its grave. All the while cleverly hiding "the body"—the knowledge that anything is in fact dead at all. Without a body, no death certificate can be signed; no crime can be said to have been committed.

- Our ability to obtain jobs, education, loans, insurance, physical security, representation; our vulnerabilities; and our rights as sovereign citizens are now being determined by data-warlords buying and selling tens of thousands of data-points on us that we don't even know exist, which are algo-rhythmically massaged into deep-profiles of "us" we can neither see nor correct, to be sold to people we do not know exist who affect our lives in a world of laws that can't protect us.

- No one is immune—the same is true for leaders.

- We are vulnerable because we share the cultural belief in the existence of privacy—and thus believe that we can do things in private that we publicly say we do not do. Examples include any mendaciousness—from hidden addictions through violent abuse to treaty violations, whether for individuals, organizations, or governments.

- Transparency—perhaps forced, perhaps logical—becomes an emergent solution, indicating that people can no longer be controlled by their own data.

- Concomitantly, citizens will become less accepting of invisibility from the data-barons, impunity from the law, or obscurity in governance.

The definition of "transparency" we both arrived at was different from most. For many people discussing mega-data's assaults on privacy, transparency is about the visibility and control of data, and about the ways people live their lives in the public realm.[3]

To the two of us, transparency instead took on anthropological overtones. When faced by massive invisible profiling that judges them as un/worthy (of financing, jobs, insurance, dignity), or that leaves them vulnerable (to blackmail, criminal attacks, social manipulation), people may resist by de-stigmatizing the negative values used against them. This may upend institutional power by showing that corporations, criminals, and governments are, in fact, nothing more than "profile-able" individuals equally beholden to the new cyber-scapes of transparency.

These are not forgone conclusions. Populaces may become

cowed and overwhelmed by the weight of such social changes, or emboldened in new ways. History has relentlessly shown that some societies falter and crumble, others muddle into mediocrity, and still others forge innovations in redressing abuses of power and justice. Neither of us found the outcomes predictable.

We didn't write anything down that day, deciding to return to these questions when the book was closer to completion. In the meantime, perhaps other, more "reasonable," conclusions would emerge.

When we sat down months later to "do the conclusion," we decided to first recap what we remembered of our summertime discussion on transparency. Lisa began speaking without interruption or hesitation. When she finished, we both sat back and nodded, and then gathered our stuff and left. She had gotten to the heart of the matter—reproducing some of the key points of our earlier conversation, adding some of her own take on things.

It seems fitting to let her unedited and unprepared words that day stand on their own. After all, it is Lisa and her generation who are the ones walking into this emergent unfinished world.

Lisa:

I feel like all of the information we get suggests that we are moving closer and closer to what we formerly thought was impossible—the perfect panopticon.

And this in itself is neither good nor bad, it's just a collection of data—data that can be used for good and bad, by people. But the nature of this information makes the implications of this very complicated. The panopticon easily can present as a tool of the state, if we don't take care to monitor this and maintain the democracy at its most fundamental and profound level.

But perhaps a new form, a new dynamic, of democracy is emerging. It's really hard in this new era of digital technology for a state to hold threat information apart from the people—especially since the people now have access to a lot of the same resources to get this data as the state.

However, this doesn't make an Orwellian dystopian impossible. You can still see a place, a world in which you live your daily life, where you are watched every day by governments and corporations—watched and regulated.

More likely, however, it seems we are entering a brave new world where we are not controlled by a single authoritarian state, but by the whims of the people. It may still be a dystopia, but one controlled by our own desires rather than someone actively suppressing us. There will not be one voice, but many different voices pulling for power.

There's also the possibility of a utopian world in which there is healthy transparency—a world where there is no room for secrecy, and where there exists a previously impossible level of honesty. Whether or not we'll be able to live in a world where everything is reported seems to depend on our ability to regulate the way this information is used, the availability of the data to everyone, and the quality of the information.

As an American I am perhaps more likely to see democracy as being more good than evil, so the cyber-based control of traditional powers over the actions of many individual actors does not, to me, flag as an immediately bad or dangerous thing. The potential for danger is clearly there, but alongside it there is also a possibility for a distribution of power that has never been there before.

This level of transparency has already been shown to be a threat to figures I would regard as oppressors—such as dictators in Egypt, Libya and now Syria. Their own discomfort with the Net seems to suggest that the Internet has the possibility for human rights and the democratization of information, and…well, everything. This is not to disregard the disquieting potential of disorder that the Internet can also introduce because, perhaps, there is a little bit of dictator in all of us—a small part of us that wants to retain complete control.

We have been taught to fear the life that is short, nasty and brutish—perhaps with good reason—and yet almost all of the most powerful nations on earth are run by the people, and order is still maintained. In places of crisis, people often respond with creativity and support—like the way the world extended voice-to-Net technologies to people when governments like Syria cut off Internet communications for their population.

It is unlikely that an extreme answer here will be the right one. An entirely unregulated Internet is as dangerous as a completely censured and regulated one.

Transparency is not necessarily just a logical conclusion from all the big data-banks and identity-information sales—for these are controlled at present by a few (and largely hidden) companies and groups. Transparency also may well be a way of combatting the purchasing and use of this personal information on all of us for everything from jobs and loans to blackmail and violence.

I think there is a joke: "It's official, you can't get away with affairs anymore—the head of the CIA just got caught and, if he got caught, anyone can."

I think the difference between blackmail and transparency

essentially comes down to accessibility. When one person knows they have control over another person—when everyone knows the secret's already out—there is no leverage.

Look at Yelp—the online site where people give their reviews of products and services. It's supposed to be helpful and a win-win situation. Businesses that do their business well will attract more business, and those who don't do as well will suffer. This is a fundamental aspect of capitalism: the power of word of mouth—the consumer's ability to evaluate quality. The problem is that this works only when the information reported is true and all biases are clear. I remember my dad saying Yelp was turning into a mob and doing shakedowns—like saying "you have to support us." Reviews are good only if they are honest; information is helpful and powerful only when it is true. Increased transparency theoretically should lead to more honesty and fairness.

But when information rests only in the hands of a few, the knowledge becomes power to be used against others. For transparency to succeed, there can be nothing gnostic—no secret divine knowledge held only by a few.

In my generation, we are beginning to become acutely aware of the impact of information. To survive and to exist at high levels of scrutiny we maintain that only we ourselves understand the whole picture and that the world at large sees only a side of us. These stupid Facebook posts, for instance, on the wall of a stranger can indict that person forever. But on our own walls, it's only a momentary lapse of judgment.

We hoard our own identity and deposit it one piece of information at a time and then simultaneously maintain that, since no one has a comprehensive picture of all of this—of us—only we can understand.

Our idea of selfhood is less secure. We are then able to undergo willingly greater levels of transparency than those before us would ever have felt comfortable with. There is the danger of no falsifiability, where no one can prove us wrong. This, however, works very well as a coping mechanism against very high levels of scrutiny. We are able to keep our "self" protected in secret even while it is attacked or analyzed by strangers.

We are aware that we exist in a world full of visibility, and we act accordingly. We pose for Facebook pictures, we publish pictures and text messages, and we network fiercely in an attempt to show we fit and belong in a bigger picture.

In addition, we are aware that our reputations spreads like wildfire and that anything we do or say to one person will be seen and heard by anyone who is relevant to our social world. These facts have become integral in our maintenance of public image. In the face of this, it's become part of the unspoken rules of friendship to support each other through social networks in order to show solidarity.

Endnotes

[1] Joel Brenner, *America the Vulnerable*, New York: The Penguin Press, 2011, pp. 163 and 210.

[2] Matt Taibbi, "Wikileaks Was Just a Preview: We're Headed for an Even Bigger Showdown Over Secrets," Taibblog, *Rolling Stone*: *http://www.rollingstone.com/politics/blogs/taibblog/wikileaks-was-just-a-preview-were-headed-for-an-even-bigger-showdown-over-secrets-20130322*. Accessed 3/26/2013. Referring to Alex Gibney's documentary *We Steal Secrets* about Wikileaks.

[3] The opposing solution is upholding an individual's privacy, either through regulation or through each citizen's own security education.

TIAGO CARDIERI INTERVIEW
PRACTICES LAW – "OMNIBUS HACKER"
HACKATHON AGAINST CORRUPTION
BRAZIL, NOVEMBER 2012

~ CN ~

"HOW MUCH DANGER is there in the digital world now?"
Danger is when you think there's danger. The most fearful thing is to fear the possibilities of acting. I know a guy who is so nervous about "the dangers" that he uses two proxies. As far as I'm concerned, it just makes his Internet slow.

The worst thing, the most dangerous thing, is to resist "bad" things—to live in fear. Keeping safe on the Internet is not something we should all have to worry about. This should be the work of someone else—people whose job it is to provide security—not those who are building and creating; not those who think about how to make the Internet more creative; not those who are looking for a third way.

"The future? Where's it going?"
When I was a student in university, I remember a professor

talking about the changes taking place in these times of transitions. He said it's not the world itself that's changing; it's not even technology per se that's changing. It's not any of these tangible things that people often focus on to explain transitions.

No, he said what's changing is the cognition of people, the flow of parallels, of language, of expression. It's a quality.

The Net is just a commodity to build so many languages. But building a new sense of cognition—well, no one yet knows what it's going to be.

Tiago leans back in his chair and looks up reflectively at the sky for a moment:

I don't know how I...I don't know how my generation sees things.

He smiles and nods with quiet confidence as he realizes his answer:

I don't think my generation cares about how people see things.

I think people have long faced a fear of being alone in their way of thinking—you know, that they see the world a certain way, believe in things that are very important to them, care about living life in a certain way, and they fear no one will understand them; worse, that no one *can* understand, and they retreat into silence.

But today, you can communicate with someone who thinks like you; you can find your community on the Internet. The freedom, the potential this opens up, is important to understand. You can think any way you want to think, and this gives you a confidence to do things the way you want to do them. There's a real creativity in this, and instead of feelings of isolation you have confidence and excitement. And you don't fear having to do this alone.

Tiago pauses, trying to find the explanation he wants, then leans for-ward bringing his two hands together to indicate that what he's about to say links up with the point he's just made.

Ok...There's an idea on the Net: "non-rival goods."

He stops, trying to figure out how to explain this. I ask him if it's the same thing as something we have in anthropology called "unlimited good," or "non-zero sum?" In anthropology, these are usually described as coming from non-Western hunters and gatherers and tribal societies that believe there is always enough for everyone, and that one person's use of resources does not reduce what is available for others. It's hard to grasp in Western thought. It is like saying, metaphorically, that you can take a piece of pie from the whole, and it does not lessen the amount available to others.

Yes, it's like that, only for digital times. Let me try to explain. It's no problem for me to make mistakes. This isn't like the past, or the hard material world. I don't have that fear of "doing it wrong."

Holding up his hand, pantomiming smoking a cigarette, he said:

Look, if I have cigarettes, I take one, smoke it, and that's the end of it—only one smoke and it's gone.

But with information, there are no restrictions. It's not possible to use up, like a cigarette. Instead, you can use information and use it again, endlessly. This is computers; this is the Net. So we don't have a fear to try things, to use things. You don't use these things up. You use them and it just keeps adding.

What does our generation care about? I said before that I didn't know, but this is it: To be happy—to do what they want to do.

A professor of mine in university once said that now it's the student who's the critic. It's an example that shows a real change in thinking, and in one's sense of power.

Today a student in school doesn't feel the need to debate what a teacher says. He doesn't stand up and protest against what authorities are saying, trying to explain out loud and to the teacher what he thinks and wants. We don't feel the need to protest against power by arguing with someone. If he disagrees with something a teacher says:

> he goes and sits in the back of the room—
>
> (*Tiago mimes moving and sitting in a new chair, sitting in a relaxed position sprawled in his chair with his legs out, as if he's in a world of his own*)
>
> pulls out his phone—
>
> (*he picks up his cellphone*)
>
> looks up information online—
>
> (*he leans over his phone surfing, as if the classroom fades into the background and he is his own teacher*)
>
> puts this together in a valuable way—
>
> (*he leans back with a smile, as if satisfied with his work*)
>
> and doesn't dispute. He just does it.

We just do it. We're less conflicted in our relations and communications. We don't have to argue against advice we don't accept or agree with. We don't have to fight for expression. Someone doesn't have to "convince me." It's losing time. And we have no patience for this. It's a waste of time. This is how we see it today.

You have access to so much dynamic information, so many dynamic things now. So for us it's: "just ignore what you don't agree with"; just go for more dynamics.

"How will all this affect the politics of states?"

The nation state will have competition. The state is a form of communication. You can say it's an object of communication to a certain degree. And look what's developing to offer new alternatives. For example, there's a new thing online: Online Dispute Resolution. If I don't like the way the judiciary is taking care of matters, I can go to Online Dispute Resolution.

Traditionally, "authority gives authority and credibility." But now, authority doesn't have, doesn't control, this credibility. Everyone can now control their own parameters. Justice, for example, isn't something that is "given" to us so much anymore. It is something we help create, we interact with.

There are so many examples like this. And they add up to the fact that the way people relate to each other and the way they look at this form of socialization called "the state" —well, this is changing. People will see it in a different way.

Is it going to be good? That's relative.

Freedom is not "good"—freedom is freedom. It's how we measure things. "Good," like "water," is an expression of yourself.

In the case of states where "freedom" means the ability of citizens to multiply the channels of expression open to them, it's like "bread"—it's a very important "good."

You can look at Shapiro's book about controlled revolution in considering all this. But it's a waste of time saying theories.

I mean, when you're talking about the state, and power, and the Internet, and the changes coming—there are people, there are businesses and governments, who will try to control the Internet, communication, and other people.

But I can't see how people can control the Net. I worked with lawyers and privacy law; I've worked or interacted with corporations,

NGOs, the government; I've been in on some of the emerging discussions on how to "handle" the Internet.

I know there are people who are trying to control the Internet. I can see the options that exist around Internet control in this new era: You can try to control and fight—control technology and fight against those who don't want to be controlled or who want to control in a different way; or you can ignore it and say: "You all, all you who want to control the business and politics of the Internet, take it—and I'll do my own thing and not fight." It's like the student in the classroom who doesn't debate with the teacher but just goes off on his own and does his own work, creates his own "good."

Because the first group can't ever really gain control—they get control (or some kind of control) and then lose it; then get it and lose it; fight, get it, lose it—caught in an endless cycle that really goes nowhere.

People in the digital culture are skeptical when people say they are going to control the Internet—the digital world. We doubt.

"Big Data and Stealing Reality?"

A while back I worked for a database company that, among other things, associates people's private information from the Net and their public records to create larger comprehensive files and analyses to sell. In companies like this, you have so much information that you can't even sell it all.

Information is different from traditional commodities. Information is never a limited good. You can sell information to anyone—but it's not gone from your possession. It's not like food—where you eat it once and then it's gone permanently, or a chair that you can sell only once, to one person at a time. You can't sell a chair to someone and they now have the chair and you still have it at the same time.

It's not the same with information. Information is an infinite commodity. It's pliable. You can sell it and still have it at the same time. You can sell the same information to another person and now all three of you have it, ad infinitum. You don't know where the information goes. It's not a matter of information itself. It's about the work the information can do—the way it works together with other information. It's a matter of associating it with other information, and the ways it can be associated and used.

"The outcomes of all this?"

Maybe people will abandon their privacy—there is a logic here. We helped a little bit to build a freedom of information act. This was a victory. We worked for this because we believed in the greater benefits of public information. Now there is a personal data protection law. It's a real accomplishment, and it was a rough road at times. People were fighting for this against some of their own friends.

This goes much deeper than the ways information can be used. These are also ontological conflicts. On one side you have the state of culpability, and on the other the state of information now. What you do with information now and what may be done in the future have to be distinguished. For example, in the future people may have to disclose whether information is public or private, and the ways in which this data can be used by third parties depends on which of these arenas it falls within. People's information may be used in more ways than they ever intended, and this then raises questions concerning the culpability of use. It brings in distinctions between public, personal, and private data as defined by the law and as used by companies in practice.

Let me give you an illustration. Say aggregated information is used in a study looking at ethnicity, economics, and payment status.

It turns up the fact that 10% of Afro-Brazilians managed payments of X-amount of money a month. This is labeled public personal information, and because it is only an aggregate—a percentage that does not identify actual individuals by name in any way—it's deemed fair use. The data is considered safe to collect, analyze, and use publicly. But what if there are only 5 black people in the city? Well now it looks like private information. Now you can identify actual people from these aggregates. You can make judgments about them based on this data, judgments that can directly affect these individuals.

Societies have evolved ideas of the definitions and the divisions of private and public information. But these ideas of public/private information are now operating in a world where information travels so fast, is so much more distributed, and so much more public. This concept of public/private information seems so natural, so instinctive—but it is also so social.

These ideas take shape and place in certain specific social conditions. But social conditions change—the ideas are not immutable. Ideas of what constitutes public and what is considered private can take on new meanings; they may be rewarded in new ways. People will have to choose how to communicate; to choose between "expression" and "fear of someone controlling you by this information."

Maybe people will behave differently when this all becomes more real to them. Maybe I'll decide to tell people what I'm thinking and how I'm behaving, maybe not. The key is this: I have the freedom to express myself as I choose; I determine what I think is the healthiest and most creative way for me to live. Expression, and thus the freedom of information, rather than fear, is valued.

But maybe because of the fear of being controlled, people will try to close access to their personal information, to keep it secret—to restrict their freedom of self-expression.

Who can say which scenario—freedom of expression or fear of control—will more likely emerge? There are no parameters to say which will win out.

And the fact of the matter is, this will not be decided with reason, but with behavior. How people actually act will bring the answers. When people make a decision, they are already practicing in accordance with that decision. Their practices determine their decisions.

And look at practice now—people are practicing without fear. They value the freedom to express themselves how they please.

Some person may say the most important thing in life is being able to express yourself and say anything and everything one wants in social media and public net-spaces—and to hell with privacy. What if that person finds out that someone is using their personal information publicly, or in inappropriate ways? What if that person didn't react by starting to stifle the way they express themselves for fear of negative consequences? What if, instead, that person used this very freedom of expression to publicly say this guy, or this company, or this group is doing something wrong to everyone? What if freedom of information is the very means to stop attempts to control people by controlling their information—the very means to stop the fear? It's kind of paradoxical.

All of this is a new thing. I don't know and, honestly, I don't even try to make a concept out of this. I don't want to get addicted to a concept.

We're DIYP: Do It Yourself People. We just now got the tools for it; we can listen to all music, get any information—we have access to anything that can be.

There's an example I really like. There's a favela in Sao Paulo where they didn't have any Internet access. So they got together and made an *intranet* for the favela with boxes of milk. It worked.

So I have a hard time understanding questions about the possibilities of controlling or collapsing the Internet. I don't really understand the common fears you hear in the USA about governments being able to control the Internet—turn it off and on—or about an attack that takes down the Internet.

"They" may "collapse the Internet," and then we'll just build a new one.

The point is, it's not about digital realities. It's not about technology. It's not about material things. It's about building up; about creating and communicating and expanding our world. It's about humans and what we do. We are making consequences in human culture independent of hardware and the material Internet. If I had problems, if I couldn't manage, I would stop paying my water bill; but I would still pay my Internet bills, no matter what. We've had a taste. What I'm saying is there's no going back. I'd do without water before I'd give up my Internet. We tasted it and we want more; so people would be real creative in making working Nets if someone tried to shut the Internet down.

There is a story about Miguel Nicolelis that illustrates what I've been saying here. Miguel Nicolelis is a Brazilian neuroscientist, and he's a Professor at Duke University now. Among other things, he's been honored as one of the top 50 scientists in the world by *Scientific American*, and was nominated for the Nobel Prize in 2009.

Nicolelis is interested in recording and understanding the language of the brain. He says you can't understand the brain one neuron at a time. It's like when you're studying a forest, you have to see the whole forest—so too you have to look at the whole brain.

Understanding the language of the brain made it possible for him to implant electrode arrays into a monkey's brain that enabled the monkey to control a robotic arm by thought alone. He went on to demonstrate that a monkey could control an independent robot by thought alone, by a brain-computer interface.

Miguel is very nationalistic. He loves the Palmeras soccer team from Sao Paulo. He may be teaching at Duke University, but he's Brazilian in the ways he sees a lot of things in the world.

One time he was on a talk show in the USA, and the host asked him: "Do you have any fears about people using your research to create robot-monkeys to go to war?"

And he answered: "We in Brazil don't think about things like that. The first thing you think about in the USA is going to war. It's kind of a traumatic society—people become their own fears; and you then don't stand for what you want, but what you fear. We in Brazil don't think like that."

This brings me full circle to my first point. Digital groups here in Brazil are happier than in the USA—because we are happy in general. We do what we want to do. What more can we ask for?

Tiago and I walked back to the Hackathon. Someone from a North-American cyber-security group had placed several little green cards printed with short cyber-safety messages on one of the tables. One said "Do you Facebook? Big Brother has already friended you." Tiago picked it up and said:

"Now the fear comes in little green cards."

Conclusion

~ CN ~

MOST OF US USE THE BOUNTY of the Internet in the course of our days without ever realizing that battles rage all around us on the Net. As we sip coffee and browse online, power in the world is being redefined, economies forged and destroyed, political wars fought, and cultures invented.

Countries with the most high-tech infrastructures are now the most vulnerable in the cyber-era: sitting ducks in the face of critical infrastructure assaults. The complicated financial systems spanning the world today leak monies and data into the cyber-shadows at alarming rates, and have little in the way of back-up plans if those flows turn into hemorrhages that shut down exchange. Our security systems can be infiltrated and turned back to spy on us in a deranged kind of panopticon. As Michael said in the opening of this book: "You can even hack the big red button."

It does little good to ask whether this is a new state of affairs or a continuation of the human condition. Both are true.[1] Battles over dominion have been fought for thousands of years, though not in global nanoseconds.

It is perhaps more useful to turn our attention to the realities of the emergent world. One of the realities virtually all security experts agree on is that the cyber-intruder, to date, has the upper hand.

As invisible as the full scope of digital-threats are to most people, some of the solutions, some of the heroes of creativity, are equally unrecognized.

One story I read in Brian Krebs' blog has stayed with me. It is a powerfully iconic example of what I might colloquially call "humans doing good for no reason at all." As with my work on the frontlines of devastating wars, it is this human capacity for creative solutions that generates the very fonts of societies and change.

Krebs tells the story of encountering twenty-year-old French hacker, Steven K.[2] As a teenager, Steven, or "Xylitol" in one of his aliases, was a respected player in the software piracy or "warez" scene—cracking popular software so people could use it for free. But in his late teens, he began to reverse-engineer the malware kits available in underground cybercrime forums. He took on sophisticated botnet-building kits like SpyEye Trojan—releasing the cracked copies of the malware for free. When updates for the crimeware were released, he cracked and released these.

For the last several years, Krebs writes, Xylitol has also been "locked in daily battle with Russian scareware and ransomware gangs." He and some of his associates crack and publish the license keys necessary to free computers taken over by these programs. At the time Krebs wrote this, Xylitol and his friends had been fighting the Russian ransomware gang "WinAd" to the degree that they were releasing codes to free victims on a daily basis—often just hours after WinAd starting using a new variant of the crimeware.

Krebs notes that there are mixed reactions to Xylitol's work cracking botnet building crimeware. Some criticize him for releasing free malware code, thereby making it more accessible than when payments are required. Others praise him for cutting into criminal's profits, showing their code patterns and trends, and taking a stand against their power.

For me, there is a deeper set of considerations. Krebs writes that Xylitol is unemployed and lives in his parents' basement. He, inexplicably, devotes most of his waking hours to fighting Russian cyber-gangs and crimeware widely affecting people.[3]

On a larger level, I question whether simple answers are possible. How do we assess the il/legality or im/morality of hactivist groups breaking into poorly secured government, business, or security sites and publicly posting their exploits? These attacks have shown that in the majority of cases, the "secure" site was woefully—and some argue, criminally—insecure. In many cases a basic "script-kiddie" level attack—an attack a teenager could learn on a YouTube video—was possible.

We, the general public, turn over our most private and important information and valuables to our governments, doctors, banks, schools, employers, insurance companies, and retailers. As Bruce Schneier[4] writes, we do so on a foundation of trust, for we are no longer able to control our own data. This trust is significant, for the data can be used for identity theft, blackmail, ransom, stalking and murder, loss of employment and finances, ad infinitum.

If the people guarding society's most valued data are negligent—that is to say, if they don't use even the basic up-to-date security that any computer user should—the endangerment to those they have a mandate to protect is serious. It is the cyber equivalent of putting one's gold in Fort Knox and then leaving the door unlocked. Where is "right" or "wrong" in this example: leaving the entry to someone else's valuables unlocked, or showing the unlocked doors by publicly breaking in?

At present, it appears many professionals will not implement adequate security unless forced to do so. In such conditions, my sensibilities lean towards knowing the vulnerabilities.

I'm not sure if anyone truly knows the full extent of cyber-threats—the full extent of the realities cast by cyber-shadows. No government, military, security or academic group can claim the paramount status of "digital-superpower." In other words, no formal institution—no governing body or security organization—as yet can muster more people and digital fire-power than the cybercrime groups on the one hand, or the sprawling leaderless "digital bands" of computer literati and hackers like Xylitol on the other.

This constitutes the frontlines. No one holds the digital upper hand: no country reigns supreme, no industry or military is invulnerable, no computer is ultimately safe.

Right now, like it or not, the cyber literati are all that exist in fighting the pathologies of the Net. Whether they are employed in formal institutions, work for governments, live in their parents' basement, or work a grub job to pay for their tech, they are the only ones with the skills to shape the digital universe and the vision of what that universe can accurately be. Some countries have already recognized this: a young hacker from Estonia I met at a hackathon told me with pride that his country is working on teaching programming and coding to every grade-school student, recognizing that digital-literacy is essential in the world today.

Governments may try to control the Internet and its intellectual property, but they are acting nationally in a global ecosystem—which makes complete national shut-down impossible. So in this curious new era, it is not the governments who regulate the moral compasses guiding the development and use of the Internet as much as they would have us believe. The architects of the Internet and the people who populate it are forging ethics and morals in practice. In real time.

So-called "white-hat hackers" lock horns with so-called "black-hat hackers" across nations, financial systems, industries, and cyber-fiefdoms. "Gray-hat hackers" are evolving new sets of morals that no one yet quite knows how to assess—from Anonymous to Xylitol. New colors are emerging. Kids in a favela in Brazil create a working Intranet from milk cartons.

Societies can rail against stereotypical "hackers," and governments can try to control the Internet, but this won't change the fact that, at present, digital literati and "netizens" are the people directing the development of the cyber-universe that defines much of our daily life.

Until general societies take more responsibility for understanding the actualities of the digital world rather than the power-laden myths and fables, the decisions are in the hands of the people who create it.

Endnotes

[1] Tom Boellstorff, *Coming of Age in Second Life*, Princeton: Princeton University Press, 2010; Bruce Schneier, *Liars & Outliers: Enabling the Trust that Society Needs to Thrive*, Indianapolis: John Wiley and Sons, 2012; Zygmunt Bauman and David Lyon, *Liquid Surveillance*, Cambridge: Polity Press, 2013.

[2] Brian Krebs, "Software Pirate Cracks Cybercriminal Wares," October 13, 2011, *https://krebsonsecurity.com/2011/10/*. Accessed 11/25/2011.

[3] People like Brian Krebs, who work (sometimes at great odds) to bring accurate information to the general public, often go unrecognized by that public. There are many such people. I was speaking recently with an electrical engineering graduate student specializing in computer security, and asked him if his cohorts are interested in uncovering some of the "shadows" in the Net. He replied without missing a beat: "Sure, everyone would love to, but a lot don't—it's hard. Look at Krebs, he's working to document global cyber-crime groups and his site gets targeted constantly trying to take him down. It's like working in a cyber-war zone."

[4] Bruce Schneier, *Liars & Outliers: Enabling the Trust that Society Needs to Thrive*, Indianapolis: John Wiley and Sons, 2012.

Conclusion
~ LC ~

HAVE WE EVER BEEN SAFE? It depends, I suppose, on what it means to be safe; if safety means making harm impossible, then no, of course not. At any given moment, nearly anyone around you could kill you if they really wanted to. It wouldn't be hard. They'd just have to pull a trigger and run. However, people do not typically panic and buy Kevlar vests every time they prepare to step outside. They know that people, for the most part, do not want to kill other people. The cyber world is no different. It seems mystical because it is not kinetic, but the same rules largely still apply. Yes, it could all collapse tomorrow, but people tend to hold it together. Community and social regulations trump legal ones. People monitor other people, and this tends to keep the system running. This does not mean, however, that we do not need the legal framework.

Currently, the Internet is largely self-governed. When you look into the existing laws, there is a surprising lack of legislation. Most of the current laws are just carried over from the kinetic world. I found it is usually not the case that there are special rules for cyberspace, but rather that the rules of the real world simply do not stop applying. It is illegal to have child pornography, whether you have pictures on your computer or magazines hidden in your basement. It is illegal to abuse animals, whether you are holding dogfights in real life or posting videos of them online. Online, the enforcement of both of these things has been surprisingly communal based. It hasn't been Uncle Sam coming in with SWAT squads. Perverted Justice is a group of thousands of volunteers dedicated to catching child predators. They have been responsible for over 500 convictions so far.

I believe that this inter-community regulation holds the key to the future of the Net. I also think we need alternatives in case of an emergency—just as a farmer might diversify his crops to protect against calamity, so too should the United States ensure that its infrastructure can operate on many different levels, both with and without the Internet. I think that education, rather than legislation, is the best way to approach cyber threats. We need offensively trained computer hackers working for the government, a more computer-literate population, and more honest dialogue about the threats we are facing. Rather than attempt to stop Internet crime through punishment and legislation, working towards a common good can obliterate the need for some forms of cybercrime. For example, piracy can be prevented if goods are easily accessible online. Hulu is a great example of this. Rather than turning to illegally torrented TV shows, people will often choose to watch Hulu and endure the ads because of the high quality and reputability of the site. Similarly, websites like Grooveshark allow people to legally listen to free music, whereas iTunes, by charging for every song, encourages people to turn to piracy. Creative Commons is another great example of this communal common good working out in everyone's best interest—people get to reproduce content, and, by accrediting the original artist, they build the reputation of the person they borrow from. The Internet, like the real world, is comprised mostly of good people. Given the option, they will consistently choose order over chaos and right over wrong. However, there has been and always will be evil. To protect against this, more sophisticated detection methods are needed. Until the problem of attribution is solved, it is going to be nearly impossible to regulate cybercrime. It is no longer easy to oppress people. Dictators cut the Internet for a reason—it gives power to the people. In the end, it all comes down to the people. Closeness is blinding, and it is easy to forget how powerful the "every person" in the everyday is.

Is the Internet good or bad? The answer, I think, is neither—it simply is. It is how it is used that will ultimately decide its impact on everyday life. So far, I think we've seen that the Internet has primarily been used for good. Communication and access to information are just a two of the multifold goods that have come from the Internet. However, it is foolish to ignore the cyber shadows—the places where potential threats lurk unwatched. I hope we as a global community can face these shadows, and work to make the cyberworld a more secure one in the future.

Postscript
~ CN ~

THE RESEARCH FOR THIS BOOK began when I inadvertently discovered the darknet. Curiously, years and reams of research later, I still hear almost nothing on the kinds of things I first saw on the un-indexed Net. The average computer security people don't seem to know much about them; the digital-literati just don't seem to talk.

This began years back when I watched a number of remote-access attacks on my computer and cell phone that continued over a long period of time. A file being dragged to my desktop and then down off the screen altogether, pictures copied to a new folder and removed, as well as weird programmatic activities. The most startling was watching my iPhone—which did not have a sim card in it—power itself on, access the Net, open Gmail, access my inbox, download copies of my mail, set mail to new, close the program and the Net connection, and (the one mistake) leave the screen blank rather than returning to my normal screen. The attack took place in several seconds, not minutes, meaning it had to be—at least in part—automated. Moreover, not only was there no cellular service connection, there was no wireless service in the area. The clincher was that I had never accessed this Gmail account on the iPhone, nor ever entered the password on the device—meaning that the intruder had gotten all this data from my laptop and linked it to my cell phone.

This was in 2009 and early 2010. When I called the police to find out what to do on the advice of concerned University of Notre Dame IT security staff, the policeman said that such attacks were impossible, therefore I was lying to them, and he hung up on me.

What makes these intrusions so interesting is that they appeared to come from a person with average computer skills. One forensic expert I spoke with explained:

> Carolyn, you keep talking about how sophisticated these attacks are. But, in fact, they're average, not from a pro. You noticed them. You'd never notice an attack from me.

People who know me asked if the intrusions might be from someone I encountered in researching political violence and crime. But the cyber-intrusions coincided with a series of break-ins and thefts in my family home—all in a small town in Iowa—likely coming from someone local and known to me.

Periodically I would find a bit of odd code on a device of mine correlating with the intrusions, and drop these into search-engine inquiries. This was how I inadvertently stumbled into the uncharted Net. The first site I found routed me to an "e-slaves site" for sale on cruises. Following these bits of code I found sites purportedly selling babies, forged customs documents, hit men, specialty sex groups, ad infinitum—as well as cyber-attack malware and hacking services. The infamous Silk Road darknet drug sales site that was taken down in fall 2013 would be considered tame in comparison with some of these sites.

One bit of intrusive code I found on my cell phone and browser begins to show the enormous scope of what is available. It led to a business website selling vehicle tracking devices, something many businesses legitimately deploy. But a careful reading of the fine print showed that these could communicate not only GPS location, as well as all sounds and conversations, but it could also covertly control car functions—from engine performance and display readings to starting or disabling the vehicle "in remote locations where there are no observers." The options continued.

Though I do not know if this is common, my point of entry was often through very innocent and generally highly boring sites—an article in a medical journal on degenerative arthritis in African-American males over 60, a long list of burial plots in a Midwest cemetery, a discussion site on autism, and so on. While looking professional, some reference, some link, some question was out of place and provided an entry point.

The list of goods and services available became so extensive that I often didn't even bother to read the details on the more common ones. Untraceable and untrackable cell phones; spyware for every brand of computer and cellphone; devices to block home and business alarm systems from working, or to take over control of the systems to turn the surveillance onto the owners; "real estate" sales beyond the pale of any law; "banking services" whose pictures of "bank employees" were all teenage women, or that dealt in monies "off all radar."

Curiously, when I found and searched the different code on different devices after intrusions, I would often encounter the same kinds of sites. Some of the different websites showed a similarity of design—as if the same software and the same set of design tastes were used. It's not a stretch to think that people would use the same products across different sites, much like GoDaddy or iWeb designs pop up around the Web, or Ikea furniture around living rooms.

It is the degree of organization, interrelated links, business acumen, and complex range of extra-legal products and services that is worth noting. Some of these sites I dubbed Web-Marts, proverbial Walmarts of extra-legality. My impression is that the mega-mart model of the material-goods world has been enthusiastically embraced in the digital Deep Web.

Answers are few and far between. My final impression of the digital universe at present is one in which struggles over power in the most fundamental sense are taking place among a vast array of stakeholders.

As myriad battles ignite over who will be the world's next legal and extra-legal hegemons throughout the world's cyber-realms, most people chat comfortably on their smartphones and surf on their computers oblivious to all of this—and oblivious as well to the fact that they, their data, behavioral patterns, bank accounts, identities, consumer preferences, political choices, and their very construction of self *are* the battleground, the resources, the spoils of war, and the harbingers of peace.

RESOURCES

Some Online Resources

PEOPLE:

Paul Asadoorian – PaulDotCom.com

Richard Bejtlich – TaoSecurity.blogspot.com

Jeffrey Carr – Digital Dao

Joshua Corman – cognitive dissidents blog

Dancho Danchev's blog

Marc Goodman – FutureCrimes.com

Jeremiah Grossman – WhiteHat Security

Mikko Hypponen – F-Secure Weblog

Dan Kaminsky's blog/twitter

Brian Krebs – Krebs on Security

Moxie Marlinspike – thoughtcrime.org/blog

Bruce Schneier – Schneier on Security

Gene Spafford – blog.spaf.us

NEWS & INFORMATION:

2600 – The Hacker Quarterly

Anonymous – AnonNews

Ars Technica

AVG Free

Boing Boing

ComputerWeekly.com

CSO Online

CyberCrime & Doing Time

CyberWarZone.com

Darknet – The Darkside – darknet.org.uk

Dark Reading – darkreading.com

efinancialnews.com

ehacking.net

ehackingnews.com

Electronic Frontier Foundation (EFF)

eSecurity Planet.com

ESET Threat Blob – blog.eset.com

Ethical Hacking

Extremetech.com

Forbes – The Firewall

Government Computer News

Hack a Day

Hack In The Box

Informationweek.com

InfoSecIsland.com

Infosecurity-magazine.com

InfoWars.com

IT-Director

Malware Domain List Forum

Malwareinfo.com

Mashable

Motherboard.com

My Digital Footprint

Networkworld.com

PC World

Reddit/technology

Red Tape Chronicles (nbcnews)

Scmagazine.com

Securelist.com

Security, Privacy and the Law – securityprivacyandthelaw.com

Security Affairs

Securitynewsdaily.com

siliconindia news

Slashdot.com

SpyEye Tracker

Synbiowatch

TechNewsDaily.com

Technology Review (MIT)

Technosociology.com

TechRadar

TED Blog

The Hacker News

Thehackersblog.com

Thehackerspost.com

The security ledger – securityledger.com

Threatmatrix.com

Welivesecurity.com

Wired

Wired / Threatlevel

zdnet.com / ZeroDay

Zeus Tracker

GROUPS, ORGANIZATIONS, BUSINESSES – RESEARCH INFORMATION:

Arbor Networks Blog
Black Hat
CanSecWest
CERIAS
Chaos Computer Club
ClubHack
DefCon
Electronic Frontier Foundation
Electronic Privacy Information Center
FireEye Blog
Fortinet Blog
F-Secure Labs / f-secure weblog
Georgia Tech Information Security Center / Emerging Cyber Threats
Reports
Guardian Analytics
Hackinthebox
HackMaimi
IEEE.org / Spectrum.ieee.org
Imperva Blog
Kaspersky Lab / Kaspersky's Security Bulletin / Kaspersky's threatpost.com
McAfee / Security blog / Threat Reports / Research
National Security Agency
Norton – Cybercrime reports
PandaLabs / cyber security blog
Ponemom Institute
Privacy Rights Clearinghouse
pwc.com
RSA Blogs
SANS Institute / SANS Internet Storm Center
The Schmoo Group – SchmooCon
Securosis / blog
Shadow Server Foundation
Sophos Labs / Sophos Labs Threat Reports / Sophos' Naked Security
Symantec / Reports / Response Blog
Taia Global
TaoSecurity / Taosecurity.blogspot.com
TrendMicro Blog
US-Cert (Department of Homeland Security)
VeraCode blog
Verizon – data breach reports

Contemporary Novels
on cyber-threats & solutions, by cyber-literati

J. C. Allen
  M.O.D.

Cory Doctorow
  For the Win
  Homeland
  Little Brother
  Pirate Cinema

Dave Eggers
  The Circle

William Hertling
  Avogadro Corp: The Singularity
    Is Closer than It Appears
  A.I. Apocalypse
  The Last Firewall

Sridhar Jagannathan
  The Cyber Mafia

Alan B. Johnston
  Counting from Zero

Matthew Mather
  CyberStorm

James D. McFarlin
  Aftershock

Ramez Naam
  Nexus
  Crux

Douglas E. Richards
  Wired
  Amped
  Mind's Eye

Mark Russinovich
  Zero Day
  Trojan Horse
  Rogue Code

Neil Stephenson
  Reamde

Daniel Suarez
  Daemon
  Freedom
  Kill Decision
  Influx